Out of the Night
Writings from Death Row

Compiled and edited by
Marie Mulvey Roberts

**with the assistance of
Benjamin Zephaniah**

Foreword by the Rt Hon. Michael Foot

New Clarion Press

First published 1994

New Clarion Press
8 Evesham Road
Cheltenham
Glos GL52 2AB

New Clarion Press is a workers' co-operative.

A catalogue record for this book is available from the British Library.

ISBN paperback   1 873797 09 5
       hardback   1 873797 10 9

Typeset in 10/12 Lucida Bright by Jean Wilson – Typesetting

Printed in Great Britain by T. J. Press (Padstow) Ltd

For Jan Arriens and LifeLines,
for Marie Deans and Sister Helen Prejean,
and for everyone on Death Row

Invictus

Out of the night that covers me,
Black as the pit from pole to pole,
I thank whatever gods there be
For my unconquerable soul.

In the fell clutch of circumstance
I have not winced nor cried aloud.
Under the bludgeonings of fate
My head is bloody, but unbowed.

Beyond this space of wrath and tears
Looms but the Horror of the shade,
And yet the menace of the years
Finds and shall find me unafraid.

It matters not how strait the gate,
How charged with punishments the scroll,
I am the master of my fate:
I am the captain of my soul.

calligraphy by Ya'qūb

— W. E. Henley

Contents

Contents

Foreword

LifeLines is the most honest enterprise I know.

It makes no promises or pretensions, but it still saves lives. Several of those whose lives have been saved or are being saved have the chance to speak in these pages. Readers will also be able to judge for themselves the quality of the writing, but, even more importantly, they will be given the chance to see what LifeLines is about, and why I make the claim about its unique nature.

I was lucky enough to have been introduced by Marie Mulvey Roberts to a LifeLines conference in London when a full-scale report was given by an expert on the Death Row situation in the United States, where the offence against human rights is most widespread. It is the campaign there that matters most. But some of those conditions prevail also in territories which have legal systems inherited from Britain.

Prison writing is one of the ways in which prisoners have been enabled to defend and liberate themselves; several prisoners have used their pens to outwit their gaolers. Marie Mulvey Roberts' *Out of the Night* has given a new range of writers the chance to show how that old tradition still lives.

Michael Foot, December 1993

Acknowledgements

Thanks must go first and foremost to all those who have contributed to this anthology. It is with great regret that I have been unable to include all the contributions received, which meant that some heart-rending decisions had to be made about what to leave out. Because of this, I intend to save the unpublished material for a sequel called *Death Row International: Rights and writers*, which will be a collection of writings by condemned prisoners around the world.

The contributions sent by prisoners have given me rare glimpses into the lives of writers existing in a situation that is unimaginable for most of us. For the last two years I have been living vicariously on Death Row. To work on this project has been an overwhelming and extraordinary privilege. Most harrowing has been when prisoners who were faced with an execution date reached out to the book as a last court of appeal.

Without the help of LifeLines, *Out of the Night* would have remained in the proverbial darkness. The inspiration and enthusiasm of Jan Arriens, the chairman, and Tori Burbridge, the forbearing editor of *The Wing of Friendship* and *The Feather*, along with the support of Sarah Girling, Jane Officer, Colin Williams, Vi Brighton, Esther Gilder and Elizabeth McOwat, have been especially welcome. Marie Deans, who is one of America's leading campaigners against the death penalty, was the first person I met when I arrived late for my first LifeLines conference in London in 1991, having just missed her keynote address. In the light of this, it seems particularly appropriate that she has given her permission for that speech to be reproduced here. Her charisma still remains with me, as does that of Sister Helen Prejean of the Louisiana Abolitionist Group known as Pilgrimage for Life, who was the original inspiration for the poetry competition from which this book arose. The book is a tribute not only to all the prisoners on Death Row, but also to LifeLines.

Since there are far more people to thank than space allows, I apologize to those whom I must leave out. My thanks go to Alan Arenstein, Amnesty International, particularly Mandy Bath, Robert Beasley (UK), Anne-Marie Bull-Njaa (Norway), Rick Halperin (Texas), Mark Warren (Canada), Rosemary Bailey, Keith Best, Tim and Mary Binder, Clare Broom, Charlie Butler, Susan Carey, Ida M. Kapel Caro, Geoff Channon, David Cohen, Marie Davies, Madge Dresser, Audrey Elcombe, U.A. Fanthorpe, Michael Foot, Sophie Garner, Marion Glastonbury, Bob Gross and the National Coalition for the Abolition of the Death Penalty, Paula Hagan, the Irish Co-ordinator for LifeLines, Maurice Hindle, Gary and Janalee Hoffman and the Rising

Son Ministry, George H. Jones and the Alabama Committee to Abolish the Death Penalty, Margaret Jones, Liz Krauss and members of the Death Penalty Information Center, Naomi Lester, Moira Martin, Brian Masters, Andy McCoy, Sue Milne of Irish LifeLines, Leanda Mounsey and her budding Young LifeLines, Mary Mulligan, Sister Mary Ninian, Brian Pattenden, Bill Pelke and Murder Victims' Families for Reconciliation, Mark Penn, John Valdimir Price, Erika Reinhold, Henney B. Rip, Emrys Roberts, Charles A. Satterfield, J. C. Smith, Joe Stern, Victor L. Streib, Jonathan Theobald, Christine Thornber, Maureen Timmins, Judge Stephen Tumim, Stephanie Wilkinson and Australians Against Execution, Mark Whiteley, Brian Williams, Alan Wills, Mandy Wise and all the others who supported this project.

On Death Row I would like to thank John Allen, Zolo Agona Azania, Umar Amin Abdullah, Jermarr Arnold, Gahiyi Bakari, Michael Bankert, Grady Bankhead, John Barfield, Lee Max Barnett, 'Black Panther' Tony, James L. Beathard, Chay'im Ben-Sholom/Marshall, Jeffrey David Brantley, John Earl Broker, George Brown, Eugene Broxton, Edoard Castro, Douglas D. Clark, Robert L. Cook, Al Cunningham, Jeffrey K. Davies, Dennis Dowthitt, Jo Duncan, David Duplantis, David Durev, William D. Elledge, Elen Ford, William Wentworth Foster, Dwight Gaines, Johnny Lee Gates, Tracy A. Hansen for being so cheerful and encouraging, J. Hart, Gene Hathorn, Ronald Hoke, Andrew Eric Huffman, Jackie Humphreys, my neglected pen-pal, for being so understanding about the time this book has taken up, James Lee Hunter, Lloyd Earl Jackson, John J. Joubert, Carl Eugene Kelly, Billy Kuenzel, Floyd Meslak, Nelson Mitchell, Mike Orndorff, James Otto Earhart, Joseph P. Payne, Randy Scott Perry, Marion Albert Pruett, Linsay Rashad, Richard Rossi, Richard Shere, Edward Spreitzer, Gary L. Sterling, Alberto Valdez, Darryl Travis Watkins, Daniel E. Webster, Jessie D. Williams, Joe Louis Wise Sr and everyone else who sent material for the book.

I would like to acknowledge the kind permission to reprint poems from *Baptism of Dirty Windows*, *Ne Déjà Vu Pas* and *Rainbow's End* written by Trovatore Poetaster, the pen-name of Ted Cole and Martin Draughon, who are Death Row inmates in Texas (available from 'Trovatore', PO Box 130031, Tyler, Texas 75713-0031 for $5.00). Tori Burbridge has generously allowed me to publish the following pieces from *The Wing of Friendship*: Tony Chaney, 'Death by law'; Douglas Clark, 'This job is killing me'; Thomas Battle, 'Silly questions'; Tim Binder, 'A priceless gift'; Mark Penn, 'A thought for a friend'; and Daniel L. Crispell, 'Life on the inside'. The West Midlands Group of LifeLines has kindly given me permission to include material from its magazine for prisoners called *Ragbag*, which includes Danny King, 'Greetings from the grave: Death Row' and the illustration by Alvin S. Loyd called 'Death penalty law'. I am also grateful to the editors of *The Endeavor* for permitting me to reproduce the following pieces: anon., 'Vox Populi Vox Dei'; Robert

x *ACKNOWLEDGEMENTS*

West, 'Executions in the USA' and 'House of Horrors'; Don McCray, 'Death watch'; Michael B. Ross, 'Does it work – is it fair?'; James R. Means, 'Behind the concrete walls'; Gary T. Graham, 'The reality of Death Row'; Harvey Y. Earvin, 'Life on Death Row' (renamed 'The emotional cruelty of Death Row'); Donna Leone Hamm, 'An eyewitness to a murder'; Ronald K. Allridge, 'A strong spirit'; and Harold Otey, 'Death penalty pilgrimage'. Brian Williams and Julian Broadhead have kindly allowed me to reprint material from *Prison Writing*, including Martin Jarvis, 'Recipe for prison pruno' and 'The scars', and Lloyd Earl Jackson, 'Wall of death'. I would like to thank Norman Mailer for permission to reproduce Gary Gilmore's poem from *The Executioner's Song* and Tracy A. Hansen for graciously allowing me to use from his book-length manuscript, *My Point of View: Capital punishment*, the following extracts: 'Application of the death penalty', 'First arriving on Death Row', 'Daily life on Death Row', 'Complaints on Death Row' and 'Officers working on Death Row'. I am indebted to the artists on Death Row and in LifeLines whose work appears in this book. The cover illustration *Original Pain* is by Terence Kelleher and most of the line drawings are by Steven King Ainsworth. My thanks go to Jacob Dougan for allowing me to use his calligraphy of 'Invictus'. The title *Out of the Night* was suggested by U.A. Fanthorpe.

Names have sometimes been changed or information withheld, usually in connection with whereabouts, for the protection of contributors. There has been a minimum of editorial interference with contributions. All material has been accepted in good faith and neither the editor nor her associates and publishers should be held accountable for the accuracy of the content of pieces submitted by prisoners. The publishers, Fiona Sewell and Chris Bessant of New Clarion Press, have been a continual source of strength, reassurance and optimism. It was their faith in this project that helped to keep it on the right course.

When this book seemed a particularly steep climb (often up an ever-increasing paper-mountain), the prisoners were unfailingly encouraging. Many would sign off their letters with the injunction 'Don't quit'. The simplicity of this advice makes it all the more effective as a motto that could be adopted by all of us in our fight against the death penalty.

Marie Mulvey Roberts, School of Literary Studies,
Faculty of Humanities, University of the West of England,
Bristol, March 1994

INTRODUCTION: SOMEONE IS KILLING OUR AUTHORS

The Governor was strong upon
   The Regulations Act:
The Doctor said that Death was but
   A scientific fact:
And twice a day the Chaplain called,
   And left a little tract.

Oscar Wilde

It was during the preparation of this book that the editor came to a fuller realization of the grim fact that the contributors were being systematically eliminated. This should have come as no great shock, since these authors are prisoners living on America's Death Row. But dealing with the practical reality of this can be very different from considering this extraordinary and incongruous factor in the abstract. From a publishing and editorial point of view, it has literally meant a life and death race against time in order to get contributions to press. Such considerations have given the term 'deadline' a sinister new meaning, since execution dates have had to be taken into account when setting up submission schedules. Preparing this anthology might have felt like participating in a macabre meta-fictional whodunit had it not been for the fact that the identity of the killer has never been a mystery.

The death penalty in America today is imposed by thirty-eight jurisdictions out of a total of fifty-three. Apart from the US government and the US military, the remainder are the so-called 'killing states'. The state which has carried out the most executions over the last two decades is Texas (66) followed by Florida (31), Louisiana (21), Virginia (20), Georgia (16), Alabama (10), Missouri (10), Nevada (5), North Carolina (5), South Carolina (4), Mississippi (4), Arkansas (4), Utah (4), Oklahoma (3), Arizona (3), Delaware (2), Indiana (2) and California (2). Other states have carried out one execution.[1] By the time these figures have been published here, they will have increased. Two-thirds of all the executions are carried out by four Southern states – Louisiana, Georgia, Texas and Florida – which are known collectively as the 'Death Belt'. What Death Row prisoners themselves feel about capital punishment and the states that carry it out is the subject of the chapter entitled 'Killing states', where they are given a right to reply.

From there the reader will be taken on a journey beginning with a capital trial, followed by an account of first arriving on Death Row and continuing with an exploration of aspects of life for a condemned prisoner. There will be reflections on what it is like to have been abused as a child, to be black, and to be a woman living on Death Row – as well as the importance of maintaining contact with the outside world. The final chapters are concerned with the trauma of facing execution and then release, either from prison or from life itself. Each of the prisoners' stories fits into a wider narrative concerning the imposition of the death penalty in the United States.

The contributors to this anthology are writers and poets who live continually under the threat of death. They are introduced to their readers not in the first instance as convicts, who have been found guilty of crimes that carry a capital penalty, but as the collective authorship of *Out of the Night*.

The idea for this anthology grew out of a poetry competition organized by Marie Mulvey Roberts in 1992 for prisoners on America's Death Row. The contest proved to be so successful that there was a demand for more. Competitions like these have been made possible only because of the networks created by LifeLines, a non-political organization founded in England which has spread to other countries, notably Ireland, and which supports and befriends condemned US prisoners. The poetry judges were fully fledged members and included the Right Honourable Michael Foot, the former leader of the Labour Party in Britain, Benjamin Zephaniah, the British Caribbean poet, U.A. Fanthorpe, another well-known poet from Britain, and Dr Rosemary Bailey of the University of the West of England, Bristol. The author of the winning poem received the Jackie Humphreys Award, named after Marie Mulvey Roberts' pen-pal, whom she visited at Oklahoma State Penitentiary in McAlester during Easter 1992. The prize money was raised from donations received at a pipe organ recital she gave in Bristol, and a recording was broadcast over a television channel for the Death Row prisoners at McAlester. A selection of poems gleaned from the competition has been included in this book, along with entries from a writing competition which she organized a year later. The award for the winner was named after Billy Wayne White, a prisoner who had been executed at Huntsville, Texas, in April 1992 and whose poem, written shortly before he died, has been printed here. The judges were Michael Foot and Judge Stephen Tumim, Her Majesty's Chief Inspector of Prisons. The prize money was donated by Billy Wayne White's generous pen-friends, Tim and Mary Binder. Their story of how they coped with the loss of someone who had become as dear to them as a member of their family moved everyone who heard it at a LifeLines conference held in Birmingham, England, in 1992, and is retold in the chapter 'The art of losing'.

It was at the same LifeLines conference that Marie Mulvey Roberts and Benjamin Zephaniah met for the first time. Both were already members of LifeLines, and their contact with prisons had convinced them of the importance of encouraging prisoners to write creatively. Benjamin Zephaniah is well known as a poet in Britain, and his poetry and performances inspire prisoners throughout the world. His first-hand experience as a prisoner made him aware of just how lonely prisons can be. By visiting and giving concerts regularly in all kinds of penitentiaries, he has helped to break through the isolation that is bred into prison life. Benjamin Zephaniah believes that creative writing, particularly poetry, can open up a path of self-reflection for the individual, especially one who is incarcerated. For offenders this can result in a rehabilitation of the will in the direction of finding new and more positive opportunities. The work that Benjamin Zephaniah has carried out in British prisons has led to his involvement with organizations outside which support prisoners after their release, such as SHOP (Self-Help Organization for ex-Prisoners) and NACRO (National Association for the Care and Resettlement of Offenders).

Like Benjamin Zephaniah, Marie Mulvey Roberts has worked for NACRO. She has taught Language and Literary Studies in UK prisons to all categories of prisoner ranging from juveniles and petty offenders to lifers, and across an ability span ranging from remedial learners to undergraduate students of the Open University. While teaching at Styal women's prison in Cheshire, she encouraged prisoners to develop their skills in creative writing. The value of providing these budding authors with an outlet for publication soon became apparent. To see their work in print, and to share it with others, was one way in which these women could collectively combat the frustrations of prison existence. Her idea for the magazine entitled *In Styal* did not materialize, however, for even though it had the enthusiastic support of the prisoners, it was never given the go-ahead by the prison authorities.

Much of the content of this book deals with strategies for coping with the ordeal of surviving life on Death Row. The chapter 'Life on Death Row' is devoted to the day-to-day endurance of an existence often in solitary confinement for up to twenty-three hours a day, in a cell which can be as tiny as 5 ft by 7 ft – a size, incidentally, that falls below the minimum recommended by the American Correctional Association. It is often seven years or more before the death penalty is actually carried out, by which time a prisoner will have exhausted the legal system of appeals. What happens next is reflected upon in some of the later chapters in the book: 'Death watch', 'The art of losing' and the grim medley of 'Songs of execution'. Reprinted here, from Norman Mailer's *The Executioner's Song* (1979), is a poem written by Gary Gilmore, the first American to be executed since the reinstatement of the death penalty during the mid-1970s, who faced a firing squad in Utah on 17 January 1977.

The subject of execution is the most painful of all to confront, and yet the fact of it is inescapable in this context. There are five methods used: electrocution, lethal injection, gas chamber, firing squad and hanging. When it finally does take place, it is staged in such a way as to mask the realization of what is going to happen. Stephen Trombley's appropriately named film and book, *The Execution Protocol* (1993), reveal how much of this is articulated through the language of a military exercise. The use of such discourse can serve to distance participants from the brutality of the reality facing them. Apart from those concerned directly in the killing and those supporting the condemned prisoner, most who are involved participate by virtue of being spectators, which, for the authorities, complies with a peculiarly American form of accountability.

Readers of *Out of the Night* will find themselves acting as witnesses in another sense, to the moments of torment and tranquillity experienced by the inner self of a prisoner facing this horrifying ordeal, rather than to any macabre spectacle.[2] Often words can be just as real and sometimes even more compelling than images. The actuality of capital punishment tends to be sanitized throughout Western culture in various ways. For example, it can be relegated by a politician to a statistic in an election campaign, deployed within the plot of a novel, used as a stylized device to mark the climactic triumph of the FBI in a gangster movie, or even presented as a topic to spark off a piece of creative writing in a prisoners' anthology. But in the final analysis it constitutes a reality, taking place in America today, which is the taking of a human life by a US state.

To associate the imposition of the death penalty with fiction or the cinema is to risk creating a sense of distance which can prevent many of us from having to think about its implications. But unlike in a film, most of those who witness an execution have literally come to see 'The End', while the preview, the aptly named 'death watch', has been seen already by the guards in the Death House. If these final scenes are actually filmed and transmitted to the public, they are presented spasmodically and rendered episodic by the rituals of appeal and stay of execution in what has become a modern-day *danse macabre*. Even more disturbingly, these images can be presented during prime-time television as a confusing hybrid of sensational journalism, soap opera and snuff movie. When the satellite pictures of the build-up to California's first execution in recent years were transmitted around the world in 1992, horrified viewers watched Robert Harris being taken in and out of the gas chamber at the whim of the Supreme Court, which had become the grim choreographer of his death. In Britain, this ghastly iconography has done more than anything else to influence public opinion against the reinstatement of capital punishment.[3] Let us hope that *Out of the Night* will continue to reinforce this message – this time not through images, but through words.

Some people would argue that, since many of our authors have themselves murdered, they should be killed in return. Such retributionists actively embrace the pragmatism of capital punishment, instead of passively evading the issues involved. They are not moved by the moral arguments in regard to legalized state killing, or by the fact that executions do not serve as a deterrent but rather can increase the murder rate. The fact that the retention of capital punishment is also an unnecessary drain on the taxpayer has failed to win the case for abolition. The cost of executing a prisoner can be up to three times more than the cost of top-security life imprisonment. In Texas, for instance, a death penalty case costs roughly $2.3 million as opposed to the three-quarters of a million dollars which would cover the cost of imprisoning someone in a single cell for forty years.[4] The motivation of those in favour of the death penalty rests on one single issue: the desire for vengeance. But should blatant revenge be the final solution of a civilized society when it is self-evident that the death penalty does not act as a disincentive, but only perpetuates the violence which so disfigures the American way of life? The deprivation of those confined within the penal death chambers is a mirror of the moral impoverishment and political paralysis which afflicts so many American citizens today. Robert Kennedy, who had good cause to reflect upon such means of retribution, declared that 'Whenever any American's life is taken by another unnecessarily – whether it is done in the name of the law or in defiance of law ... in an attack of violence or in response to violence – the whole nation is degraded.'[5]

When the death penalty was reinstated in the 1970s by a Supreme Court ruling,[6] it was in contravention of several amendments to the US Constitution. In the case of *Gregg* v. *Georgia* in 1976, the Supreme Court ruled that the death penalty was exempt from the Eighth Amendment of the Constitution, which forbids cruel and unusual punishment. This controversial interpretation effectively removed constitutional safeguards against the imposition of capital punishment and opened up the floodgates for state killings. At present there are approximately 2,750 Death Row inmates, who include thirty-three women. Nowadays, executions are carried out with such frequency that they are rarely reported in the international press. The United States is one of nine countries which carry out two-thirds of the world's judicial executions,[7] and except for Turkey it is the only member of NATO to impose the death penalty.

What is not so widely known is that the United States is one of seven countries that execute juvenile offenders, and in the last decade only Iraq and Iran have put more to death than has the USA. Amnesty International employed shock tactics in its campaign against this practice in America, using the slogan 'Sending children to the electric chair'.[8] The imposition of the death penalty on juveniles is in direct violation of the decrees of human rights organizations worldwide and of international standards on capital punishment, including resolutions taken by the United Nations and the Geneva Convention of 12 August 1949. More than ninety juveniles have been sentenced to death since the reinstatement of capital punishment. There are currently thirty-three Death Row inmates who have been sentenced as juveniles (some of whom have contributed to this book) and eight have recently been executed.[9] Of the thirty-six 'killing states', twenty-four permit the imposition of the death penalty on minors, and eight states have no minimum age limit. This means that, technically, children of any age can be executed.[10]

The majority of states that impose the death penalty apply it to those suffering from physical and mental illness or impairment. Bill Clinton, while he was Governor of Arkansas, ordered the execution of Ricky Ray Rector even though this prisoner had a seriously limited mental capacity. He was so severely brain-damaged that he had received an operation which was interpreted by some as the equivalent of a full frontal lobotomy. The effects and implications of this surgery were hotly disputed at his trial. Despite these mitigating circumstances and a personal appeal made by Jesse Jackson, Governor Clinton refused clemency. He even left the presidential election trail and returned to the Governor's Mansion to ensure that the execution went ahead. Opponents of the death penalty devised a slogan along the lines that Clinton was dying so much to be President that he was prepared to kill for it. Clinton's support for the imposition of the death penalty is expressed in a letter reprinted in an appendix to this book.

On 24 January 1992, at Cummins Prison, Arkansas, Ricky Ray Rector was given a lethal injection. This method of execution is even more of an affront to medical ethics than the others, and it is by no means more humane, since the regulations insist that prisoners must be physically and mentally aware of the process towards their death. In this particular case, the execution went horrifically wrong and witnesses outside the execution chamber heard moans while medical technicians tried frantically for an hour to find suitable veins into which to inject the poisonous substance. They attributed their problem to the prisoner's prescribed medication of mellaril, an anti-psychotic drug, and to the weight he had gained while on Death Row. In order to try and overcome these problems, the condemned prisoner is reported to have assisted the execution team in their task. As far as the executioners were concerned, it was imperative that the execution was carried out before midnight, otherwise it would have been automatically postponed and thus would have inconvenienced the waiting President. In order to speed up the process, a paramedic slashed the prisoner's arm. This brutal process is known as 'the cut-down method', which is a term taken from active combat and illustrates how language can be used as a distancing device. What happened to Ricky Ray Rector is indicative of the horrific effects that an ambitious politician can have on an individual. It is ironic to consider that a President from a town called Hope also shares his name with a prison called Clinton, where one of the first electric chairs was installed during the last century.[11]

In the jurisdictions with the death penalty, eleven mentally retarded or mentally ill offenders have so far been executed. The states which forbid the executions of those suffering from mental retardation are Georgia, Washington, Maryland, Kentucky, New Mexico and Tennessee. The first paralysed person to be executed after executions resumed was Charles Stamper, who was electrocuted on 19 January 1993. The image of him being lifted out of his wheelchair into the electric chair graphically illustrates the correlation between caring and cruelty that is written into the execution protocol. Consider the irony of the prison doctor who must run a medical check on inmates who have been transferred to the Death House to see if they are fit enough to die.

The extracts from prisoners' letters reproduced by Jan Arriens in his book *Welcome to Hell* (1991) offer a moving and powerful insight into the living nightmare of those who exist on Death Row. *Out of the Night* is a return visit to this dystopia and once again lets us hear voices from a terrifying darkness. The importance of these two books is that they give prisoners an opportunity to communicate with the outside world that can often lead to dialogue. The idea of reaching out is explored in the chapter 'Going home in a dream', while those on the outside are able to respond in 'Outsiders reaching in'. The juxtaposition of these chapters is intended to represent the communication seeping in and out of the prison walls – a form of photosynthesis that brings transformational light into impenetrable darkness. The positioning of these chapters is significant since they lie at the heart of the book, where they can convey more effectively a metaphorical clasping of hands between those outside and those within.

Even though prison writing is a well-established tradition, there have been few outlets for prisoners wanting to publish their work. The new British journal, *Prison Writing*, along with the Canadian *Journal of Prisoners on Prisons* and *Prison Journal* are welcome responses to this need. On a larger scale, the publications of Amnesty International provide a forum for prisoners of conscience, many of whom are professional writers and journalists. Effectively these are POWs in a war of ideas and the world has woken up to their plight. But as regards those awaiting execution on US soil, few prisoners today are likely to arouse the outcry that followed the sentencing and subsequent execution of the Rosenbergs, who were put to death in 1953 after being convicted as Soviet spies. For most of the occupants of America's Death Row, the offences committed have been those not of ideological dispute, but of criminal action. We must not overlook the fact that some inmates are, in fact, innocent. Others have been executed solely for legal technicalities – for no other reason than that the law must follow its course. This can take place simply because crucial and sometimes indisputable evidence testifying to the innocence of the condemned prisoner was not filed by the defendant's attorney by a given date. For example, in Texas all new evidence in a criminal appeal has to be lodged within thirty days of the original trial, otherwise it is not admissible.

Of the innocent and the guilty who end up on Death Row,

many are there because they have suffered emotional and material deprivations, including the lack of educational and financial resources necessary for an adequate legal defence. Many attorneys are reluctant to carry out work on Death Row because of the inadequate pay, unwieldy case loads and social stigma, which in a few cases has led to death threats. The death penalty is often imposed not upon those who have committed the most heinous crimes, but on those who could not afford a good lawyer. These social injustices are compounded by eight states who refuse to hire lawyers for Death Row convicts, however poor or needy they may be. For these reasons, the earnings from this book will be donated to the Andrew Lee Jones Fund. This is a charity set up by Jane Officer for the purpose of supporting individuals studying Law in the USA with the intention of practising in the field of capital defence. An effective outcome of this trust fund would be to assist those who are unable to afford the expensive legal costs involved in an appeal against a capital conviction.

The observation that prisoners are invariably deprived individuals is in no way to exonerate those who are guilty. It is instead to recognize that there is a well-established correlation between the development of tendencies towards criminal behaviour and a social background of deprivation and abuse. Much attention has been given to the victims of crime, yet it ought to be remembered that 90 per cent of the inhabitants of Death Row have been victims too, of one sort or another, at certain times in their lives. The chapter 'Child abuse and warnings to the young' contains insights into how crime can become a violent transference to someone else of the abuse suffered by the perpetrator. For some of the contributors to this chapter, writing about experiences of abuse has proved to be therapeutic. Apart from opening up such opportunities for self-reflection and expression, the experience of Death Row is one of profound deprivation in every way, which reinforces the existing sense of victimization.

The number of victims of violent crime is often compounded by the imposition of the death penalty itself. The families of condemned prisoners, by becoming victims themselves as a result of suffering the loss of a relative who has been executed, have much in common with the family of a murder victim. Some of the material in the chapters 'Visiting time: love and friendship' and 'Women and Death Row' is devoted to these overlooked victims of capital punishment.

Blacks suffer most all round, in that they are victims in about 50 per cent of the murders in the USA and yet only 6 per cent of the executions carried out involve crimes with black victims. Violent crimes involving white victims are generally regarded as more serious and are more likely to incur the death penalty. One crucial factor within the American judicial system is that the system often allows the prosecution to exclude black jurors in cases involving black defendants. Some of the effects arising from the racism that can so disadvantage blacks and people of colour is explored in the chapter 'Lynching in the 1990s'. This title is suggestive of how the death penalty as an institution designed primarily to protect whites is a sublimation of the appalling legacy of the days of slavery and the emergence of the Ku-Klux-Klan. Politicians running for office have been known to make election promises to increase the number of executions, and display pictures of condemned prisoners on their campaign posters. The number of black faces that appear is calculated to appeal both to the murderous instincts of the electorate and to their racism.

Once in prison, inmates can be victimized not only on the grounds of their colour, but also because of their race, ethnic background, sexual orientation or gender. For the thirty-three women who inhabit Death Row, there is even greater hardship due invariably to discrimination and greater segregation. That most violent crimes are committed by men against women and that the death penalty is acted upon mainly by men against other men has important implications for masculinity and male social conditioning which warrant further investigation.

When one considers that the majority of the contributors to this book have had to overcome problems induced by poverty, abuse and neglect, and the disadvantages of having had little training or encouragement to write, their literary achievements are all the more remarkable. Obviously there are those who have been highly educated or are self-taught, and who have shown themselves to be skilled writers. Yet to continue the process of learning and studying can be difficult in prisons, where access to books is often subject to draconian restrictions. The availability of books and writing materials, and the opportunity to correspond and engage in creative writing, can make life more bearable for all prisoners, especially those on Death Row.

This anthology is a testimony to how prisons holding capital offenders can also be sites of artistic inspiration. The act of writing is invariably both liberating and empowering for prisoners, particularly those in solitary confinement, on Death Row or sentenced to life imprisonment. Writing can open up a vital channel of communication to the outside world, which may even become two-way through letter writing as organizations like LifeLines have shown. Among the writings collected here are sobering accounts of life on Death Row and in the American prison system, which are intended to warn young people who may be attracted to crime of what could lie in store. But throughout this book, contributors have had another didactic purpose – to register their resistance and protest against the death penalty and the states that carry it out. We should never lose sight of the power that such writing can exert in bringing about changes in public opinion and political convictions, even when these are enshrined within legislation.

One of the greatest poems about capital punishment was written by a convict and helped change attitudes which eventually led to the abolition of the death penalty in Britain. This is Oscar Wilde's 'Ballad of Reading Gaol', verses of which are quoted at the beginning of chapters.[12] Although it was composed in 1898 by a prisoner of conscience, who had been incarcerated in an English prison for two years because of his homosexual practices, it still expresses so much that is meaningful to those who are in prisons around the world, awaiting execution. Most poignantly, Wilde tells of the last days of a condemned prisoner and of the hellish silence of confinement in a prison which houses a place of execution. He talks of how prison can kill compassion and humanity by turning hearts to stone, if 'by all forgot, we rot and rot'.[13] It is to this darkness, which he describes as the 'midnight always in one's heart,/ And twilight in one's cell',[14] that we must listen, and continue to respond to the never-to-be forgotten voices coming to us from out of the night.

Notes

1. See *Facts About the Death Penalty*, 25 August 1993, published by the Death Penalty Information Center, 1616 29th Street, NW, Second Floor Washington, DC 20009.
2. Sister Helen Prejean does both in her inspiring book *Dead Man Walking: An eyewitness account of the death penalty in the United States* (New York, 1993).
3. Polls taken at the time indicated that the majority were opposed to capital punishment. Even when surveys have shown that most people would support the reimposition of the death penalty, Parliament has taken the lead and the issue has never been put to the country in the form of a referendum. See Harry Potter, *Hanging in Judgement: Religion and the death penalty in England* (London, 1993).
4. Ibid., p. 4; see also Amnesty International's *United States of America: The death penalty – briefing* (October 1987), p. 18.
5. Quoted in *The Voice*, published by Murder Victims' Families for Reconciliation, vol. 11, no. 1, 1992, p. 5.
6. The current death penalty era started when new death penalty statutes were passed after the Supreme Court's decision in *Furman* in 1972, which overruled existing statutes. Sentencing began in 1973 under these new statutes, which were recognized formally in 1976.
7. Amnesty International lists these countries as China, Iran, Malaysia, Nigeria, Pakistan, Saudi Arabia, Somalia, the former USSR and the United States. Since February 1990 executions in South Africa have been suspended.
8. *The Voice*, vol. 11, no. 1, 1992, p. 6.
9. Amnesty gave me the latest update at the time of writing on 18 August 1993.
10. Much of what Oscar Wilde said about the incarceration of children within adult prisons, in a letter to the editor of the *Daily Chronicle* dated 27 May 1897, applies to the imprisonment of juveniles on Death Row today. See Oscar Wilde, *The Soul of Man and Prison Writings*, ed. Isobel Murray (Oxford, 1990), pp. 160-1.
11. See Stephen Trombley, *Execution Protocol* (London, 1993), p. 18.
12. See Wilde, *The Soul of Man and Prison Writings*, pp. 169-89.
13. Ibid., p. 188.
14. Ibid., p. 187.

For Man's grim Justice goes its way,
  And will not swerve aside:
It slays the weak, it slays the strong,
  It has a deadly stride:
With iron heel it slays the strong,
  The monstrous parricide!

Oscar Wilde

Death by law

There are over one million men and women in prisons all across the United States of America. These prisons are overcrowded warehouses for human beings, who sit day after gruelling day, sometimes locked in small cages twenty-four hours a day, only to be let out once or twice a week for a shower. Programmes are minimal or non-existent at best and, at worst, there is terrible cruelty, both physical and mental. Those prisoners most mistreated are housed on Death Row, waiting to die by electric chair, gas chamber (cyanide poison), firing squad, lethal injection, and yes, they still have hanging in some states. (In a study conducted by Amnesty International it was discovered that in the past seventy years of executions in the United States, twenty-six men executed by various states were later found to be innocent of all charges.)

(Journal entry, 9 June 1988: 'Every day cuts into my belly like a sharp knife. The question is not why, but how can I go on living? What makes me struggle for one more breath, one more heartbeat? A stranglehold on life at this point seems so foolish. Anger is a brother I know too well!')

Death Row is the ultimate prison, the ultimate human degradation and in most states Death Row inmates are legally treated as if they are already dead. The formal prison name for a Death Row prisoner is 'condemned inmate' and in many prisons everywhere they walk a guard will precede them shouting, 'Dead man walking!' Many Death Row prisoners are not even eligible for their prison's most meagre privileges, amenities and services and consequently most days are spent sitting with nothing at all to help pass the time. Some Death Rows do allow reading, watching television and talking with each other, but there is almost never any physical contact allowed whatsoever.

(Journal entry, 29 May 1988: 'Getting up each and every morning is a personal battle, a war that, as I go to sleep each night, is uncertain whether it will be won the next day. Life is

a conflict even for those on the outside – for me it is a deadly contest.')

Death Row living conditions are such that they create men who are afraid, vulnerable, angry and alone. They live anxiously in the shadow of a faceless executioner, hoping and praying for relief while dreading the terrifying prospect of an appointment with death. Every day brings a new assault on their senses and a compounding of a fear that pervades everything they do. When they pray, think of their family or do anything, they are always aware of their status as living, breathing dead men. The state in all its power has declared itself at war with them and only their death will satisfy the law. Being secluded away from public view with little or no outside contact incites, indeed virtually guarantees, abuse and the ruthless disregard for their lives and well-being by the guards. Even the most severe and rigorous mistreatment of them will bring no action by the prison administration or the public at large. After all, they are already dead in the eyes of the law.

Alvin S. Loyd, Louisiana State Prison, Angola

(Journal entry, 27 April 1990: 'When the Dragon lurks around your door, day in – day out, smiles become very important, taking on lustre and quality. Special is a word to encompass the universe. All the special people who write and support cannot be told just how wonderful they are, it would be like shouting in Church.')

If they were men before they came to Death Row, a year or two of living there has completely taken away their humanity. Some prisoners become confused, forgetful and depressed, showing all the signs of mental atrophy. All men need to give and receive love and on Death Row there is none. They are physically and emotionally cut off from anyone who loves them and it leaves them dead inside and caring little for themselves or others. After coming to Death Row most lose what family they had because their families cannot stand the thought of waiting for a loved one to die in such a horrible manner. As a result, before their bodies are actually killed they suffer a kind of social death, slowly dying from inside themselves as they are worn down by the extreme emotional stress that is Death Row.

(Journal entry, 19 July 1990: 'The Dragon will not die! It has no name, sitting as it does the Dragon takes on a lifeforce, it is a wound that will not heal. On waking the image of the Dragon as a life/thing is strong, when really it is the grinding, eating machine of a society in the throes of madness. By decree of the faceless state the Dragon eats men!')

America is a modern nation that leads as the standard bearer of freedom and human rights worldwide. They are first in line when the time comes to condemn a third world country for the abuse of its people's basic human rights. If you are against the death penalty, and I hope that you are, I hope that you will take the time to write and ask the United States to follow the guidelines it sets for other countries in the humane treatment of all prisoners. Tell them that the destruction of a portion of its own citizens is not the answer to social illnesses. There is already too much war, killing and other barbaric acts without the active participation of a government in them.

(In the desert
I saw a creature, naked, bestial
who squatting upon the ground,
held his heart in his hands,
and ate of it.

I said, 'Is it good friend?'
'It is bitter – bitter,' he answered;
'But I like it

Because it is bitter
And because it is my heart.')

Stephan Crane

Despite the dismal conditions on Death Row all across America there is a bright hope today. Like a light on the distant horizon people in LifeLines are helping us more than they can ever know. Cut off from friends and family, the weight of state-sanctioned death on our shoulders, a letter from someone can take us out of these terrible places for a few moments in time. It is in those moments that we live again.

Tony Chaney, Death Row, Arizona

Application of the death penalty

The court: 'Do you have anything to say before I pronounce sentence?'
The Defendant: 'No sir.'
The court: 'Very well. Based upon the jury verdict of guilty and based upon the sentencing verdict of the jury, I do hereby sentence you to suffer the penalty of death in this case.'

This is what was said in my case. The words may be said more or less eloquently in other cases, but the meaning is the same – the state plans on killing you. Though it would seem this sentence is provoked solely by a crime, such things as geography, public response to the crime, prosecutor discretion, background life of the defendant and politics play a major role. All these additional factors combined create a legal system that demands a sentence of death more than the direct facts associated with the crime committed.

I don't mention discrimination to negate the life value of

any victim, in any way, but only to demonstrate the prejudicial application of capital punishment.

The gap between average defendants and jurors may not seem so large, but there's a gap no less, and this is a prejudicial strike against the defendant. Add to this that a potential juror cannot sit on the jury panel if he/she says they wouldn't vote to kill someone, and this strike is more prominent. This jury panel will not amount to a fair cross section of the community as guaranteed by the US Constitution. It would be unrealistic for the defendant to insist on twelve convicted felons, and just as unrealistic for justice to sit twelve members of society so foreign to the defendant, thus less inclined to overcome preformed bias against the defendant by lack of personal understanding.

Capital punishment is far from equally applied to defendants or crimes: I personally watched a black man sit in a courtroom and laugh over the judge sentencing him to seven years for beating another black man to death with a 2" × 4" board. It was one black man killing another black man over drugs and no one really cared about the case. I have a friend who was convicted for three execution style murders. Over twenty million dollars was involved with his arrests, he has a very precious family who spoke for him at trial, and some of the best lawyers in the country who kept him from the death sentence in all three murder convictions. Someone I once knew used to be a very famous law officer who was later convicted for two execution style murders over drugs, and suspected as a participant in several other murders. His past status/connections with the side of the law may have played a strong role in him avoiding the death sentence in both murders. Another man kills and rapes a baby girl and is given thirty years. The list is endless, and all these crimes are committed in states with capital punishment. Another infamous man confesses to seventeen murders and wasn't sentenced to death because of his geographical location in the country at the time of the crime.

I don't argue that crimes such as the ones mentioned above are deserving of death. I don't attempt to argue that such crimes aren't devastatingly heinous, but I do argue that all men and women on Death Row are entitled to enough understanding as to not be killed. And this understanding shouldn't depend on race of defendant or victim; personal family support; wealth to provide legal representation professional enough to prevent the imposition of death; past occupations or political connections; or geographical location at the time of the crime. The application of capital punishment is discriminatory in many shades – the reason for application not being what the judicial system claims.

Jesse Jackson once responded to the issue of capital punishment by saying a leader sometimes has to go against public opinion to do what is right. I strongly agree as I watch our nation's leaders try and tell the public what they want to hear rather than what is right. Application of capital punishment in America is because the leaders of the nation follow misunderstanding in the country rather than leading the country out of it.

Tracy A. Hansen, Death Row, Parchman, Mississippi

The fair and impartial trial

A rich man stood before a Court of Law
  found guilty of murder for his gain
His lawyers and doctors all gathered around
  to describe why his victim had been slain

As the judge and the jury all listened on
  the police told their obvious tale
And the decision was made that the person he slayed
  was the one who should be in jail

The next case was called and a poor man walked in
  his lawyers all paid by the state
The witnesses he called were not in the room
  but the judge said the case could not wait

The jury all napped as the state made its case
  its witnesses all called in a row

The poor man looked around the room with a frown
  at the things his lawyer didn't show

He knew his was weary of public defence
  and his caseload was way overrun
He didn't have time to check the whole crime
  he just wanted to get the case done

The papers all said his client was dead
  so he didn't really see any use
The jury said guilty so why drag it out
  by a showing of constitutional abuse

The judge rose from his bench and looked round the court
  and said we're all getting tired of this crime
I know that you're broke and probably don't vote
  so it's useless to just give you time

The state's spending money to give you a trial
  and your lawyer is just wasting his breath
I don't really know if it's right or it's wrong
  but this court now orders your death

You have a right to appeal and I guess that you will
  so I'll let those others decide
but from what I can see as for our society
  it will be better off when you've died

Danny L. King, Death Row, Mecklenburg, Virginia

Recipe for prison pruno

Take ten peeled oranges,
Jarvis Masters, it is the judgement and sentence of this
   court,
one 8 oz bowl of fruit cocktail,
that the charged information was true,
squeeze the fruit into a small plastic bag,
and the jury having previously, on said date,
and put the juice along with the mash inside,
found that the penalty shall be death,
add 16 oz of water and seal the bag tightly.

and this court having, on August 20, 1991
Place the bag into your sink,
denied your motion for a new trial,
and heat it with hot running water for 15 minutes.
it is the order of this Court that you suffer death,
Wrap towels around the bag to keep it warm for
    fermentation.
said penalty to be inflicted within the walls of San
    Quentin,
Stash the bag in your cell undisturbed for 48 hours.
at which place you shall be put to death,
When the time has elapsed,
in the manner prescribed by law,
add 40 to 60 cubes of white sugar,
the date later to be fixed by the Court in warrant of
    execution.
six teaspoons of ketchup,
You are remanded to the custody of the warden of San
    Quentin,
then heat again for thirty minutes,
to be held by him pending final
secure the bag as done before,
determination of your appeal.
then stash the bag undisturbed again for 72 hours,
It is so ordered.
re-heat daily for 15 minutes.
In witness whereof,
After 72 hours,
I have hereon set my hands as Judge of this Superior
    Court,
with a spoon, skim off the mash,
and I have caused the seal of this Court to be affixed
    thereto.
pour the remaining portion into two 16 oz cups.
May God have mercy on your soul,
Guzzle down quickly!
Mr Jarvis Masters.
Gulp Gulp Gulp Gulp!

Jarvis Masters, Death Row, San Quentin, California

Ronald Keith Spivey v. The National Rifle Association of America

I am the NRA Member Number BRB 3001 C.

I joined the National Rifle Association for one reason: to call attention to its selfish actions and complete lack of concern for thousands of people who die annually from gunshots. The NRA lobbies against any form of gun control. Handguns especially need strict licensing laws and controls.

I have been under psychiatric care since age eleven. I have been in the Georgia State Mental Hospital four times. I have spent half of my life in prisons. In 1965 I was diagnosed as a person with severe emotional problems who, under prolonged stress, goes into psychotic rages.

There should be no legal way for me to buy, borrow, trade for, or be given a handgun or any other gun. In the winter of 1976, my wife left me and took her three daughters by her first husband and our one-year-old daughter. My world was in ruins. The pain and depression was beyond belief. I started drinking to numb the pain, and this led to losing a fine franchise business. I took tranquillizers, trying desperately to fight off the soul-numbing depression. Three days after the most lonely and miserable Christmas of my life, I was taking tranquillizers and drinking all day. I had a confrontation with three men. One became physically aggressive. I just snapped and went completely out of my mind. Because I had a handgun when I went berserk that horrible night of December 28, 1976, a true American hero lost his life. Officer Billy Watson, a 14-year police veteran, was moonlighting at a shopping center to earn extra money for his wife and children. During that night of madness I shot five total strangers, and two died. I caused great suffering and emotional trauma to others that night as well. I have been on Death Row for 13 years. My guilt and the horror of that night have haunted me constantly. This prison; nothing on Earth; no one, can punish me like my conscience has done. Without a gun, I couldn't possibly have done those terrible things. Somehow we must wake up and see to it that laws are passed to rid us of the millions upon millions of guns in our society and see to it that no more are carelessly sold in the USA. We need a licence to fly a plane, to drive a car, even to fish. We should have one to own any gun, even a shotgun or rifle. Each gun sold in the USA should be sold only to someone with a licence obtained from the local police department. Before any licence is given, a background check has to be done on the buyer. The expense of this can be covered in the licence fee. Only registered licensed gun dealers should be able to sell guns of any type. A private citizen should have to sell through a dealer or the local police.

No firearm of any sort sold to a private citizen should hold over six shots. No firearm should be owned that can fire more than one round per trigger squeeze.

Anyone caught selling, trading, lending, giving, or in possession of an automatic weapon such as a machine gun or assault rifle should be charged with a felony. If convicted, an automatic fine of $5,000.00 per weapon and a 10-year sentence, with a full 48 months minimum to serve, should be mandatory. It can't be probated or suspended.

Congress should pass a law that any private citizen must obtain a licence to own any firearm and show good cause as to why a handgun is needed. Handguns should be allowed to be owned only by those who can show a compelling need.

Defence of the home and family can be done with common hunting weapons such as a shotgun or rifle. Congress should set a date as a deadline for all firearms in the possession of private citizens to be licensed and registered, or possession is a crime.

No honest, mentally healthy citizen should be denied the right to own a licensed shotgun or hunting rifle to hunt with and protect the home, family, and property. No licence should be possible for anyone under any circumstances to own a machine gun or assault rifle. There should be a fine and prison sentence for anyone who doesn't have a licence. And a second offence should have a severe fine and prison sentence.

Any crime committed with a firearm should have an additional 10-year sentence, consecutive to and in addition to any other sentence. The 10-year firearm sentence can't be probated or suspended. These laws and conditions may sound severe, but they make sense and are desperately needed. It is as easy for a felon to buy a gun in most states as it was for me to buy an NRA membership from Death Row.

Anyone wounded by an assault weapon or handgun, or the relatives of anyone killed by them, should sue the NRA for all its high pressure lobbying. That has prevented reasonable laws from being passed to regulate and control these weapons. Make them spend some of their lobbying funds defending themselves. The NRA is callous. It deserves a lawsuit each time some precious child kills himself or herself or a playmate with a firearm such as in the heart-breaking rash of child killings this past year in Florida. No matter how insane or evil anyone may be, simple common sense tells us they can't do as much damage without a firearm as they can with one.

There are paramilitary hate groups training with assault weapons and machine guns in various parts of our country. God only knows who these hate groups will focus all that firepower on eventually. Laws are needed to make this illegal and take these guns away from organized hate groups bent upon mass destruction and slaughter. The police in this nation are truly a thin blue line who stand between law-abiding citizens and total chaos and carnage in a society saturated with drugs and guns. The police do a nearly impossible job that would be made easier and safer if sensible firearms laws and regulations existed. I don't know the actual numbers, but each year many of these brave professional men and women dedicated to protecting your very lives are killed because guns are so readily available to anyone in our country. A citizen's right to bear arms was given in a time when the central government couldn't afford to maintain an army in case of war. Now we have a well-armed police, armed forces, and National Guard. So the original intent and purpose is non-existent now. Licensing and registration of guns are desperately needed. Our country has become an armed camp from coast to coast. God bless Sara Brady and others like her. She is truly concerned and courageous, and I applaud her efforts.

Each American should call or write to their Congressman and Senator and demand that he or she introduce legislation of this nature or support it when it's introduced by others. The average citizen has a weapon all politicians fear: it's your right to vote for those you approve of. Vote for those who show concern for the lives of everyone, and vote against those who gave in to the NRA and its high pressure lobbying tactics. Get together and form political action committees.

During my 13 years on Death Row, I have had nightmares over what I did. The guilt is overwhelming, and I am haunted by what I did in 1976 and hated for it too. This article will bring even more hatred aimed at me. But it so desperately needed to be done. It's a small part of an enormous debt I owe society that can't be paid in a thousand lifetimes. I hope and pray my efforts here have made each of you more aware of the insanity of a nation senselessly armed to the teeth with thousands dying each year from firearms.

We owe it to ourselves and we need to love one another enough to see to it that laws are created that will rid us of this proliferation of these instruments of death. I beg you to take action now before a distant national statistic becomes a very real personal tragedy.

Ronald Keith Spivey, Death Row, Jackson, Georgia

Vox Populi Vox Dei
(The voice of the people is the voice of God)

I am society's collector of debts and my purse is the bottomless maw of time spent insatiably storing the payment of days, implacably totalling the months and the years.

I am the abode of hope become hopelessness, of routine so deadly that even the simple act of living becomes a weary and numbing task.

I hold within me men who cling to life when even to hope is futile, men who walk my stone and concrete walled corridors in silent resignation in passive waiting.

I hold some who have long been forgotten not only by a world callously indifferent, but by their own wife, children and family as they face no other future but that of a grave, starkly numbered in a barren cemetary.

WHO WILL HIDE A NATION'S SHAME?

Who will hide a nation's shame?

We cannot eat what a burning-Bush has fed

Little wonder we are cripple and lame.

This nation's vision and sight lost, has no aim

The street child daily begs for bread

Who will hide a nation's shame?

To this low state we all came;

Indeed, our future has been sorely bled

Little wonder we are cripple and lame.

Our Mouse, sold abroad is dying the slow death of an old French dame

But no tears for hungry homies in front of the White House, shed

Who will hide a nation's shame?

Men, far away over-seas, even now plot this nation's gain

Its progress alas, rides a lead-sled

Little wonder we are cripple and lame.

Oh putrid past, to our future, lays bitter, though just claim

Exhume, one and all of us, from the abyss of greed and dead...

Who will hide a nation's shame?

Little wonder we are cripple and lame.

Brandon Astor Jones

I hold within me the confused, the perverted, the rebel, the lost and the unlucky. I hold the deprived, the misguided, the liar, the cheat, and the murderer; these too are mine.

I hold within my unfeeling walls and bars the flawed, the inoperable, the unfinished; the malformed works of an imperfect civilization.

I hold within me men who not long ago knew peace and freedom, the keenly crisp, biting freshness of a winter's night, the welcoming laugh of a child; men who now only know the rendering pain of utter desolation.

I encage not only the tired old man, but sadly, the tired young man; the blindfolded eyes of justice are truly unseeing.

Come, come and look upon the face of these I hold and see thereon the reflection of my image that is engraved as deep and final proof of society's inadequacy, of man's inhumanity.

Then you can judge the humanity of a society by entering the gates of its prison. For I AM THE PRISON.

I am the bitterness in the hearts of the many who become mine; not only the guilty, those who committed the crimes in society, BUT also those that were found guilty only because they stood alone, poor and naive.

I am the contempt of all who have learned with the disillusioned knowledge of experience of the crushing machinery of the real justice system, where a man's life and his future, his freedom, his liberty can be bought and sold, and that justice is neither noble nor just.

I am the eroding cynicism of the many who heard these men presuming to pious infallibility, as they passed judgment on them, the fallible.

I am the enthusiastic prosecutor who uses facts of innocence or guilt only as pawns of indifference to be interchanged as verbal volleyball to enhance his conviction record and promotional career.

I am the guard, a good and loving father, a good citizen, but whose sadistic acts are not accounted within my walls.

Come and look and see that I am even more formidable than my concrete and stone walls, and steel bars, and lethal gun towers; for not only do I confine, I slowly and irrevocably destroy the souls and spirits of those I hold within me.

I am loneliness and heartache that burns like ice and my teeth sink deep into the very souls of men I hold within me.

I am bleak emptiness wherein feeling is a sickness bone deep, where anxiety swells and thrusts, and uncertainty constricts and stifles.

I am the memory that comes violently in the night like the tearing screams of a trumpet sending forth from the orchestra of frustration, futility, despair, and crushingly impenetrable indifference only to be heard echoing down the dark night's concrete corridors of man's failed attempt to muffle his crying.

I am the infinite abortive dreams of numberless human failures, the holder of countless stories experienced, never shared, never told.

YES, I am the literal prison and never can my viciousness be truly portrayed. To know it, it must be felt, it must be endured.

Always I am cold and harsh and merciless for I am the intolerant conscience of an unconcerned, jaundiced-faced society.

At times I am vibrant with contempt for that lost and groping mass stirring aimlessly within me, continuously growing by the day.

Then I see one head lifted and in that face, raised to the free and open sky, I see exposed the very soul of man. Then I know that it is I that should not exist.

I am the faces in the visiting room searching; I am the grown man's eyes as they swell and fill with tears as they watch his family walk away for the last time.

I am the tautly stretched face of the man in prison khakis remembering the past warmth of his wife's touch, his children's tenderness; now his only family being the pigeons he feeds and talks to each morning.

I am the gut searching anguish that destroys the man who waits daily with silent desperation and hope for the letter that never comes, the visit that never arrives.

I am the deeply etched face of those who wait and wait, their only sustenance heartbreak, disappointment and veiled regret.

YES, I AM THE PRISON, wherein the smothering confines of a steel cage inexorably crush with the weight of human reality, wherein the endless emptiness of the day and the shattering lonelinesss of the eternal night repeat my message ... E-N-D-L-E-S-S-L-Y.

Anonymous Death Row inmate

Cell Block Six – Death Row

Far behind these prison walls and steel gates,
Are armed officers trained by the state.
There's conflict going on, silent and unseen,
With walls three feet thick to conceal the screams.

Many try to display a smiling face,
To hide the pain of this place.
So many feel brought to their knees to cry,
But one learns to remain strong – or die!

And even if you hold on, you'll lose anyway,
Because most will be strapped in that chair on execution
     day.
The politicians say it's what the public wants and never
     sigh,
Because they say the public wants 'an eye for an eye'.

Where once there was one,
A second will die before you are done!
Where once there was one killer,
Now there are three ...
The murderer
The state
and you and me.

Why should we live when another has died,
Don't you know that only God can take 'an eye for an
     eye'?

We live in our self-righteous world made of glass,
Condemning one another while we hide our own pasts.
Under the guise of 'Justice' we kill ...
While fanatics claim it was God's will ...
We cover his eyes so we won't feel the shame,
Of killing a man who's little more than a name ...
Then back to our homes and snug little lives,
We sleep without conscience next to our wives.

There's so much we can learn from the men on the Row,
So much they could teach us that we need to know.

Richard Rossi, Death Row,
Arizona State Prison, Florence

Does it work – is it fair?

The most common justification given for capital punishment is that it is a deterrent to murder. But anyone who offers this rationale is making a gut-level, emotional response without stopping to confront and thoroughly think through the issues.

Many studies have attempted to link capital punishment and homicide rates. They report overwhelming evidence that capital punishment has no effect on murder rates. There is no significant difference between the murder rates of states with active capital punishment systems and those of demographically similar, non-capital punishment states.

Outside the United States the vast majority of developed democratic countries already have abolished the death penalty. Many boast murder rates significantly lower than our own.

For example, Canada abolished the death penalty for murder in 1976. Yet last summer Prime Minister Brian Mulroney pointed out in a speech to the House of Commons that in the 10 years following abolition the homicide rate in Canada reached a 15-year low.

Internationally, the United Nations has concluded, in a report for the Congress on the Prevention of Crime and the Treatment of Offenders, that 'despite much more advanced research efforts mounted to determine the deterrent value of the death penalty, no conclusive evidence has been obtained on its efficacy.'

This, among other considerations, led the UN General Assembly to affirm that member states, 'in order to guarantee fully the right to life, provided for in Article 3 of the Universal Declaration of Human Rights', should seek to progressively restrict 'the number of offences for which capital punishment may be imposed, with a view to the desirability of abolishing this punishment in all countries'.

Still, regardless of what the studies show and what knowledgeable people say, many continue to insist that a system of 'kill and be killed' is a deterrent. But they assume that a murderer thinks as they do, clearly a mistaken assumption.

There are basically two types of murder: premeditated and emotional. In a premeditated murder the culprit either doesn't expect to get caught or, much rarer, doesn't care if he is. He expects to get away with the deed because of good planning and/or lack of evidence. Or he doesn't care if he's caught because he feels so strongly about his actions that he's prepared to face the consequences. There can be no deterrent value in a punishment that one doesn't expect to receive or doesn't care about.

In a spontaneous, emotional murder, logic doesn't even come into play. One doesn't think of being caught, nor does one consider the consequences of one's actions. Emotion clouds the thought process; the individual is not acting on something, but rather reacting to something. Emotions diminish the capacity for reason, and in the heat of the moment the capital punishment factor becomes a non-factor. Fear of death, in itself, will not prevent this type of crime.

Politicians may leap at the deterrence argument, because it sounds tough on crime, but it actually detracts from the real work of developing genuine programs for crime prevention and control. As such, the death penalty becomes the perfect political red herring – a program that sounds effective and creates a false sense of security, but in reality saps our resources.

There are acceptable alternatives to capital punishment that are more in line with the values of our supposedly enlightened and humanistic society.

The state is supposed to be the pillar of our ideals, and its institutions should emulate the best values of our society. And aren't the greatest of these values our compassion, our concern for human rights and our capacity for mercy? By conducting executions under the guise of deterrence, we are undermining the very foundations of our greatness.

There are suitable alternatives. Individuals who are a danger to society must be removed from society – there is no question about that. If rehabilitation is not possible or is not a consideration, that removal must be permanent. Society demands protection and has the right to be protected.

Those who favor abolition of the death penalty do not advocate releasing convicted murderers into society. The choice is not between the death penalty and release, but between the death penalty and life imprisonment. Life without parole, or natural life, fulfils society's requirements.

Of course, some will protest. 'Why', they ask, 'should the tax-payers pay for the prison sentences of lifers?' Even setting aside the moral arguments, there is valid reason.

A study done by the New York State Public Defenders Association found that a death sentence would cost $1.8 million, more than twice the cost of life imprisonment. And while these figures may vary from state to state, studies consistently show that a life sentence is cheaper than pursuit of a death sentence. The appeals process, long and arduous, is extremely costly.

Another argument often advanced in favor of capital punishment is that it is 'a just punishment in kind'. But we have to distinguish between society's need for 'justice' and the crime victim's desire for personal retribution. We don't burn the arsonist's home, rape the rapist, or steal from the thief. Obviously, the form of the punishment must adhere to, and be limited by, a society's standards of decency. While 'punishment in kind' may sound good, it is seldom justice in fact.

And what about the argument that dangerous individuals must be executed not only to protect society but also to safeguard prison personnel and other inmates? Only those who are unfamiliar with the corrections system, or who have not thought through the premise, can make such a claim.

Prison is designed for dangerous and violent individuals, with guards trained to handle volatile situations and policies designed for protection. For example, here at Somers, violent prisoners can be put on 'Class A' status, with 'restraints for all movement outside of cell, including exercise and showers'.

In addition, Death Row actually increases frustration and anger and stimulates thoughts of violence. This is because Death Row inmates do not serve prison sentences but merely are housed in prison until execution. Rehabilitation is irrelevant for condemned prisoners, and they are more strictly confined than other inmates. They have no access to prison work, vocational training, or group educational programs. They are typically confined for many hours each day alone in small, poorly equipped cells, with limited occupational facilities or opportunities for social contact with other inmates. Many correction officials would agree that this type of isolation, coupled with inactivity, is a breeding ground for frustration and violence.

And prison officials will tell you that men serving life sentences are generally less of a management problem than the balance of prison population. For lifers, the prison essentially becomes their home, and they want nothing to rock the boat. The fewer problems they cause, the fewer problems they have. In fact, inmate violence is much more closely correlated to age than it is to offence.

By replacing capital punishment with a guarantee that offenders will not be released, you eliminate the perceived need for the death penalty while greatly diminishing society's desire for it. The public is interested not so much in the death penalty per se as in a guarantee that individuals will not be released to repeat their crimes.

A poll by the Institution for Social Inquiry at the University of Connecticut confirms this point. Sixty percent of those interviewed said the death penalty is appropriate for those convicted of killing in cold blood. But 56 percent favored abolishing the death penalty if it could be replaced by a life sentence without parole.

Perhaps the biggest question concerning capital punishment is one of equity: Are we capable of fairly and justly imposing such an extreme and irreversible measure?

Historically, the death penalty has borne unequally and unjustly on the poor, on minorities and on the oppressed. The many inequities in our judicial system are magnified in capital cases. When an ultimate and irreversible penalty can be imposed, society must vigilantly see that justice is done. Yet in the emotional turmoil that surrounds capital cases, fairness and justice often take a back seat.

One inequity between defendants is their financial status. If you have money you can employ a better attorney. I'm not talking about buying your way out of a case; I'm talking about employing skilled and competent counsel – perhaps the most important factor in the outcome of a trial. Should the defendant pay with his life because his lawyer was outmatched?

Another inequity among defendants is based on race. In *McCleskey* v. *Kemp*, the US Supreme Court found that racial discrimination exists in capital cases. Justice Lewis Powell Jr, writing for the 5–4 majority, found that 'defendants charged with killing white persons received the death penalty in 11 percent of the cases, but defendants charged with killing blacks received the death penalty in only 1 percent of the cases'.

The court agreed that there was a risk that race may have been a factor in McCleskey's death sentence, but the majority held that the defendant failed to prove purposeful discrimination. The 'wide-ranging arguments that basically challenged the validity of capital punishment', added the Court, should be presented to the legislative bodies who are better qualified to weigh and evaluate the statistical studies.

In a dissenting opinion, Justice Harry A. Blackmun was outraged by 'McCleskey's proof that the race of the victim is more important in explaining the imposition of a death sentence than is the factor of whether the defendant was a prime mover in the homicide'. Also in dissent, Justice William Brennan said, 'We have demanded a uniquely high degree of rationality in imposing the death penalty. A capital-sentencing system in which race more likely than not plays a role does not meet this standard.'

If we cannot impose the death penalty fairly and equally, do we have the right to impose it at all?

Ignoring the broader inequities for a moment, let's concentrate on the individual case. In every court a case is supposed to be judged on its facts. Emotion has no place in the courtroom. You convict a person on the facts and you sentence on those same facts.

However, capital cases tend to be sensationalized and highly charged affairs. Emotions do make it into the courtroom and into the jury's decision, especially when one side or the other attempts to use emotions to cloud the factual issues. Should a man be executed when the jury ignores the facts and rules instead on emotion?

There are too many questions about capital punishment for

us to continue to impose such an extreme irreversible measure. Too many problems have to be resolved, too many questions need answers and too many issues need to be addressed. Rather than relax and take comfort in the illusion that capital punishment works as it is supposed to, we need to wake up and boldly address these matters.

Michael B. Ross, co-founder of Endeavor,
Death Row, Somers, Connecticut

Death Row USA

To get to this place
What do people do?
Why follow the state
Which give lessons how to!?!

Cast into this
Sheer political abyss
By those screaming voices
   Of our night
With their endless echoes
   From our darkness
Yet still reflecting
   On the light!

Being in chains
Wherever we go ...
'Tis the price we all pay
To have these death rows!

Timothy Bunch

Timothy Bunch was executed by the State of Virginia on 10 December 1992. The family of his victim had publicly forgiven him and their appeal for clemency was denied.

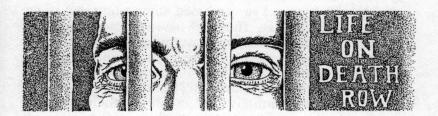

LIFE ON DEATH ROW

The most terrible thing about prison life is not that it breaks one's heart – hearts are made to be broken – but that it turns one's heart to stone.

> I know not whether Laws be right,
>   Or whether Laws be wrong;
> All that we know who lie in gaol
>   Is that the wall is strong;
> And that each day is like a year,
>   A year whose days are long ...
>
> Each narrow cell in which we dwell
>   Is a foul and dark latrine,
> And the fetid breath of living Death
>   Chokes up each grated screen,
> And all, but Lust, is turned to dust
>   In Humanity's machine.

Oscar Wilde

First arriving on Death Row

Most people are transferred to Death Row immediately after receiving the sentence of death. This transfer is one of the hardest times to deal with. Though there's an instinctive capability to survive what we face in life, part of this involves suffering much pain. I've witnessed some who seem to go insane to some degree. Though I haven't experienced this personally, not consciously anyway, this seems to distort the mental reasoning so the painful realities cannot fully dawn on the conscience.

Why is this transfer so painful? The person is wounded mentally and emotionally, yet, while at their weakest moment, they're in need of strength they don't possess, or strength that is distracted. In other words, pain is directly inflicted, and the pain attacks the capability to deal with it. All forms of pain are crashing in at once and the person is placed in a cage on their own. Rage may be added, but at this point, most are too exhausted to experience rage.

The person now sits in a cell without anyone to talk with or anything to do, trying to find a first impression, as a lead in how to deal with the situation. If a person strikes you when you first meet them, you know to deal with them with caution; if a person greets you with sincere kindness and respect, you trust you can deal with them with the same. Coming to Death Row you are faced with an empty cell that offers little lead. You wait for something to happen and that may determine the next couple of years of your life: if the first person is a chaplain offering you a Bible, you may seek answers and build hope in religion; if the first person is someone offering you some marijuana, you may find relief and determine your fulfilment dependent on marijuana; if the first person is a psychiatrist offering you something to help you sleep, this may become your sanctuary. The list goes on. It can be anything from immature behavior or arguing with whoever will holler back at you, to a television or a radio. The fact remains, you instinctively hunger for relief and wait for a first impression to start you on your way.

This is a time to hug deeply as possible – a time to overcome pain in true ways to provide clearer reasoning, to help loved ones overcome pain – a time for understanding that allows giving to be true so it can provide true comfort. This goes for the one sentenced to death, and for their loved ones.

At this stage of my sentence I concentrated on the pain of others, and how to comfort them. This kept me from crying *poor me* to the degree of adding pain to them. As they heal, I find my pain healing with them. This may not work for all, but it can work for some.

We receive by what we give. This is a time to give love and let it heal the pain. We don't have to look for happiness; we eliminate the pain and happiness will find us.

Tracy A. Hansen, Death Row, Parchman, Mississippi

Lee Max Burnett, Tamal, California

Kicks

new prison boots black arrived
though worn sometime by someone else
before i put them on
i notice the fake steel toes

of cardboard
the cracking polish on plastic leather
the brandly-newly in bold white lettering 12E
above the oil-resistant soles
the overly-abused shoestrings
i say
should i wear new socks or old
to sport them through
thick and thin
orthopaedic inserts or dr scholl's cushions
bounce off my toes or roll off my heels
and what shall i believe when
my feet are itching

Harold L. Otey, Death Row,
Nebraska State Penitentiary, Lincoln

Behind the concrete walls

The smell of overcooked beans hit Larry Murphy when he entered the chow hall. He looked around at his new surroundings. On both sides of the chow hall were tables that sat four. Something is oddly out of place, he thought. But what?

His stomach growled as the slow moving line put him in front of the steam table. He looked up in surprise when someone said, 'Larry, is that you?'

'Rock, what's going on, man!' he said, happy to see a familiar face. 'What are you doing here?'

Rock stood behind the steam table picking his teeth with a wooden match stick. 'I've been here the last ten years. The question is, what are *you* doing here? When did you get in?'

'Yesterday – brought twelve years with me.'

'That's a bitter pill to swallow, man.'

'Keep the line moving,' an officer bellowed. 'You got a problem with that, boy?'

'No.'

'No what, boy?' he said, walking up to Larry.

'No, I don't have a problem with that.'

'Oh, you don't like to say *sir*, huh, boy?' he said, yanking Larry in the chest of his shirt. 'Well, I got a trick for you. Come with me.'

'Officer Hoss,' Rock said. 'Give him a break. He's my cousin,' he lied. 'He's new. He didn't know.'

'You better tell this boy something about me, you understand?'

'Yes sir,' Rock agreed.

'And you, you better call me sir when you talk to me, boy. I'm only lettin' you make it 'cause I've known your cousin a spell and he's a pretty good ol' boy. You got that?'

'Yes sir,' Larry answered.

'Good. Now get out of my face.'

Rock came from behind the steam table to sit with Larry. When they sat down, Larry realized what was so odd in the chow hall.

'Hey, man. How come the Whites sit on one side of the chow hall and the Blacks sit on the other?'

'That's just the way it is, Larry.'

'Great. I can see this is going to be fun. First I get mugged by some guy for nothing. Now I find I've been thrown back twenty years to the 1960s in the middle of segregation.'

'You can sit over there if you want. It just isn't done that often. And Hoss only did that to you because he knows you're new.'

'Is that the kind of reception I have to look forward to?'

'You're not in the Royal Hilton, Larry. This is prison. Don't expect the red carpet treatment.'

'I don't. I just want to know if all of the officers are like Hoss?'

'Most of that sort is gone. But there's still a few.'

Finishing his lunch, Larry picked up his tray and stood to leave.

'Hey, where you working, Larry?'

'Shoeshop.'

'A partner of mine named Diamond works there. Get with him. Tell him you're my cousin. He'll look out for you.'

'All right, Rock. I'll talk to you later.'

'Yeah. Easy.'

When Larry got to the shoeshop he asked around for

Diamond. He found him in the back of the shop behind some boxes, doing pushups. As Larry approached, Diamond stood. His heavily muscled body made two of Larry's.

'What can I do for you, little brother?' he asked in a heavy voice.

'Are you Diamond?'

'Yeah. Why?'

'I'm Larry Murphy,' he said extending his hand.

Diamond went back to his pushups without shaking his hand, but kept his eye on him. 'Like I said, what can I do for you?'

'Rock told me to look you up.'

'You know the Rock?'

'Yeah. He's my cousin.'

Diamond stood again, this time extending his hand, smiling. 'Okay, little brother. Lot of nutcases around here. Can't be too careful. Yeah, me and the Rock go back a long way.'

'You been here long?' Larry asked.

Diamond looked at him with amusement in his eyes. 'I can tell you haven't.'

'It's that obvious, huh?'

'Yeah. You don't go around asking how long a person's been here or what they're here for. Good way to get hurt.'

'Just for asking someone that?'

'Here, you mind your own business. Your life could depend on it.'

Larry said nothing.

'Anyway, I've been here seventeen years.'

'Seventeen years?!' Larry asked in disbelief. 'At one time?'

'Yeah, at one time. I wouldn't be stupid enough to come *back*.'

'Seventeen years,' Larry said again. 'That's more than half my life.'

Diamond wiped his brow and gestured to Larry to have a seat on the box next to him. Larry then noticed the tattoo of a panther on his left forearm.

'Listen, man. I did six years on Death Row before my sentence was overturned. The time I've been in population has been a cake-walk compared to that.'

Larry wanted to ask Diamond what he'd done that he had

to give seventeen years of his life to pay for it, but thought better of the idea.

'I've seen a lot of guys come and go and come back again. It's like a rubber band, little brother. You stretch it one way, and when you let it go, it always comes back.'

'The guards here treat people like animals,' Larry said. 'After being treated like that, a guy can't help leaving here bitter and coming back because of it.'

'Uh-uh. I know there's guards like that. But they don't bring guys back here. Guys bring themselves back.'

'Why're you taking their side, man?'

'I'm not. I'm telling you how it is. You don't know this place the way I do.'

'Yeah, and I hope I'm not here long enough to find out.'

'I was locked down for twenty-three hours a day in a closet-sized cell for six years. You know what that can do?'

'No.'

'But you do know pressure can bust a pipe, don't you?'

'No doubt about it,' Larry answered.

'Well, now you know why guys have hanged themselves and cut their wrists to come from under that kind of pressure.'

'I don't think I could do something like that.'

'You never know, little brother. Places like this do strange things to people.'

'I still don't think I could do it to myself or anyone else.'

Diamond pulled a pack of cigarettes from his shirt pocket, lit one and offered the pack to Larry.

'A few years ago, there was a stabbing or killing nearly every day. It's not as bad now, but it still happens.'

'Yeah, Rock was telling me about that. He said guys have been killed because they changed the TV in the middle of a program.'

'He wasn't lying to you. That's what I mean. This place does strange things to people.'

'I hear you, Diamond. But why are you telling me all this?'

'Why do you think the Rock sent you to me?'

'I don't know. He told me you two are tight and that you'd look out for me.'

'We're tight,' Diamond said. 'But he knows I'm going to give it to you straight and won't let anything happen to you.'

'Oh, righteous?'

'Yeah. I came through the hard way. But you don't have to. If you leave here the way you came, learn from bitter experience and stay out, then my time with you was well spent.'

The supervising officer walked to the back of the shop with a clipboard in his hand. 'Diamond Murphy,' he called. 'The delivery truck's here. Come help unload it.'

James R. Means, Death Row, Huntsville, Texas

An endless few feet

We tread a narrow cage
Talking from fence to fence –
   thinking 'freedom!'
Stars gaze through steel mesh overhead,
Silent witnesses to a battle for space,
   and space,
Between these mindlessly shuffling warriors
Of private battles long lost.
Warriors in white, dancing to the noisy/silent
   cadence of a prison beat.

Men whose hearts and minds reach out
Where hands and feet can't go –
Marching, trudging an endless few feet –
   not even a stone's throw.
Night or day, rain or cold,
What's sought is a distance – a silence
Where our dreams can grow and unfold.
Yet even in the depths of our dreams
We're never allowed to forget the foe –
Ne'er even a moment or so.

Men dressed in gray –
To most it's just a job,
And then there are others –
Men who take perverse delight

In displaying their sadistic humor
To a captive audience.

During the deepest, darkest
      times of oppression
The 'being' of a man
      can go one of two ways:
He can build a cage within a cage –
Restricting himself only to what
      he can see, hear or touch –
Or he can delve deep within,
Exploring his innermost heart and mind;
For a man's heart, his mind,
      can never be caged.
Yes, they have my body,
This vehicle of flesh and blood which,
Minute by crawling minute,
Carries me toward the arms of fate.
But 'me' they'll never control –
      I won't let them!

Each day I witness the followers, the weak;
I feel a great pity for them,
Yet within a heart calloused by
      insult and scorn
I sense a shallow indifference
Created by the tough, unyielding world
      I now live in.
Pity, although unwanted, I can show ...
Compassion, that I must measure out,
      carefully and meagerly –
In my world it's a weakness,
      and the weak ...
The weak aren't very well off.
As in any jungle,
The weak are fair prey
      to any and all predators.

I know I'm lucky, or blessed,
To still have a strong, vibrant mind,
But it often seems much easier

> To drift aimlessly through the years,
>   as so many around me do,
> Without even the desire to change;
>   to learn, and grow.
>
> I put these thoughts into words,
> Just hoping to show a self-righteous society
> That I'm not the animal they say I am.
> My poetry – won't you let it touch your heart?
> All I want is to make a new start.

Trovatore Poetaster, Death Row, Huntsville, Texas

Just another day on Death Row

Being a Wednesday, it was like any other day behind the walls. Routine – same as the day before.

5.45 a.m.: You hear the coffee–milk cart pull into the quad lobby. Guards pushing it are hatless. One has a cigarette in his mouth. Other one has a dip of snuff and a styrofoam cup in his hand. With his free hand he grabs a coffee pitcher and sets it on the floor.

One guard bellows out, 'Coffee, milk.' Those who aren't awake on their concrete bunks begin to stir, hearing the sounds of cups being placed in the $4\frac{1}{2}$ inch by 15 inch bean holes. The entire cell house is underground and sounds bounce off the walls.

Here comes the snuff-dipping guard, coffee pitcher in one hand and spit cup in the other, hollering out, 'Coffee, milk.' He pulls up to one cell door before realizing he's standing in front of the death watch cell door. And, guess what? Nobody's home in there. He laughs to himself, then hollers out, 'Coffee, milk' again as if slopping hogs.

At your door, as he peeks in to see where you are in the cell, he puts a spit cup to his lips and spits. He pours a cup of coffee, then steps to the next cell. The guard pouring milk is pushing the cart around, screaming, 'Milk out cups in the doors.'

Now comes the chow cart with trays made by SIPs [inmates

participating in the prison's boot-camp program]. Who knows if they've passed health inspections? A guard is pushing a box with wheels, and trays of food are on the inside. He stops and shares a joke with the control room guard. Five minutes pass. Their laughter is clearly heard throughout the enclosed cell house. Must of been real funny. The guard with the chow cart has no hat on. He crushes out his cigarette on the floor and starts passing out trays. 'Pork or no pork', he says at each cell door. The door to the food box is wide open and the rest of the chow trays are steadily getting colder.

Finally, he pulls up to my cell. Same thing, 'pork – no pork.' 'Pork,' I say, knowing it's actually 70 percent soybean and only one-half cooked. Whatever is on the tray is cold by now. The light bread has got stiff; gravy has grown a skin over the top, it's so cold. There is a jag of peanut butter mixed with something so as to stretch it and make it go further. It's hard and greasy as you roll it around on the tray. Forget trying to spread it. You only end up tearing your bread to pieces. Thankfully there's some oats in another corner of the tray and after eight years experience, you know there's a chance it may still be warm in the center. Forget melting butter. Won't happen.

So that's the way you start your day in a cell on Death Row behind 'The Walls' of McAlester, Oklahoma. Light bread, oatmeal, cup of milk and coffee strained through your teeth for cigarette butts or pieces of snuff. It's a Wednesday just like any other day. They all start out the same way.

I roll up a Bugler and have a smoke to go with the coffee, which has a Kool-Aid taste because the container it came in had Kool-Aid in it the night before. Do they ever wash those containers out from one meal to the next? Who knows? I pour the rest of the coffee out, and heat a cup of water for a decent cup of coffee. Taster's Choice. I make up the bed, and grab for socks and shoes. Got early yard period for one hour, 8–9 a.m.

Around 7.45, a voice comes over the intercom rear of cell: 'Going to yard?'

'Yep.'

Voice goes, 'Be about 10 minutes.'

You get your yard clothes ready and wait for the door to

roll open, leaving the cell in your underwear, shoes and socks. You walk to the control room lobby for your clothes and shoes to be shook down by guards for weapons and contraband. One sees a handkerchief in a pocket and says, 'What's that?' I pull it out and show it to him. I offer to hand it to him and he pulls his hand back. Direct contact not allowed. You get dressed and walk to the yard, 15 feet away.

You get yard five days a week, one hour a day. It's called a yard but is actually a 30-foot walled cage with six gauge wire criss-cross across the top. It's the only place a prisoner can get fresh air. The first breath after 66 hours of lockdown is a guaranteed eye opener. The yard is 20 feet by 20 feet, five prisoners on yard at a time.

It's supposed to be a recreation time. Only thing is there is no recreation, no weight machines or free weights, no dumbbells, no speedbags, no heavy bag, no basketball goal or even a chin up bar. General population and PC (protective custody) have these things but not Death Row prisoners. In January '89, two brand new weight machines were purchased to add to the free weights already on DR yards. All the weights and new machines were taken away that same month. New weight machines were taken to general population yards.

Back to the present. In one corner of the yard exists this: Various pieces of metal welded to each end of a bar that can only move straight up and down. It is unadjustable to a person's body. No one can use the scrap iron contraption. Even the unit man couldn't get his body in position to lift with it. It has been on the DR yard almost a year with spider webs growing on it as no one has ever used it. (In the same space, a multiple position weight machine would fit.) Death Row prisoners have absolutely no recreation at all. The hour for yard recreation is spent pacing back and forth like an animal in a zoo or walking around the 20 foot by 20 foot boxed yard.

This is punishment in itself for the human body deteriorates when major muscle groups go unused. One guy lost a leg while on DR due to lack of circulation and even now is partially paralyzed.

Punishment set by the courts was death. Until that time, the DR prisoner should receive all the privileges general population gets. We are discriminated against because of our sentence, resulting in cruel and unusual punishment. Surely, as human beings, we are afforded the same rights as others behind prison walls across the USA. Oklahoma DR prisoners are not and the psychological–physical strain placed upon us borders on being sadistic.

You pace back and forth as there's no recreation. Some prisoners' mental state only allows them to shuffle back and forth, talking and mumbling to themselves. You come in off the yard with the last gasp of fresh air in your lungs, and count in your head the hours until you get your next breath of fresh air.

You walk back to your cell as you came out of it. Take your time, there's no one to talk to. The guards stay in the control room and there's 2½ inches of pipe bars between the control room lobby and where the stairs are located.

Get in your cell. The door slams shut behind you. A voice comes over the intercom: 'Got a visit.'

You change into prison blues, run a comb through your hair then beat on the cell door to get the control room guard's attention to pop open the cell door. You walk to a sliding gate made of 2½ inches of pipe bars. Walk through it and the control room guard pops one of four doors to a closet-size room without any ventilation at all. Loved ones include a nephew who's holding a phone waiting to hear your voice on the other side of security glass and steel bars that make up the visiting window. Visits are non-contact even with your own family. The nephew is 8 years old. The prisoner has never had the chance to hug him and hold him in his arms. Cruel and unusual punishment – especially so when you've not had but one write-up in 8½ years.

The new prison doesn't allow visitors to buy coke and candy bars for themselves or the prisoner they've come so far to see. The nephew remembers the old visiting room and being able to buy coke, candy; being proud of himself for giving the food to a guard so he could give it to his uncle. He saved up some change just to buy his uncle a coke, but this new prison doesn't allow visitors to buy anything. First he's confused, then he is sad. For all the years of his young life, it was part of the routine when he come to see his ol' uncle.

Voices echo where the visitors stand and sit, taking turns speaking over the phone; looking through the wire-enclosed glass and trying to see one another's eyes through the squares of steel bars. It's extremely noisy on the visitors' side with four people trying to talk at once; they aren't separated from each other like the prisoners are. They hold the phone in one hand with a finger in the ear of the other. The nephew soon gets bored. Nothing to do. No colouring book and crayons. Just gray concrete walls, a bunch of adults all talking at once and his uncle on the other side of glass and bars, who winks now and then at him. They drove 175 miles one way just to visit and conditions are pitiful.

Everyone tries to put up a front that everything is alright when what they'd really like to do is just hug one another. But, unlike California and other Death Rows across the USA, Oklahoma is non-contact. The two hours are up. The nephew is asleep on the concrete floor. The prisoner stands there waving good-bye to those who came so far just for a two-hour visit. The visitors stop just before going out of sight. The sister blows a kiss to her brother, who catches it. They grin together and she walks away so her brother won't see her tears. The last face the prisoner sees is his nephew's face, just above his daddy's shoulder, and the little hand waving bye-bye.

The control room guard pops the visiting room door and once again you are faced with the reality of a gray-walled cell block. You make your way back to the cell, the faces of those who travelled so far to see you still fresh in your mind. A voice comes over the intercom: 'Lawyer visit in 10 minutes.'

Just enough time to roll a Bugler and boil a cup of water for coffee. You do a few stretches to limber up after the visit with loved ones, thinking of them on that long road back home after stopping at a store where the nephew gets to buy a coke.

You gather up legal materials, then write down a few notes and questions to discuss with the lawyer. Be sure to take some writing paper 'cause visits with lawyers are non-contact. You have to discuss your case over a phone with an intercom in a room directly connected to the control room, where your conversation can be monitored by guards. The questions between the prisoner and lawyer have to be written out, then held up to the window and bars in order to be read and be answered. The cell door is popped open. You go to the room at the end of the staff office. Your lawyer is on the other side of the glass with bars over it, holding a phone in his or her hand in a 3½ foot by 5 foot cubicle. The prisoner picks up the phone. His voice echoes off the walls. The lawyer winces realizing everyone can hear his voice. The conversation in no way can be confidential or private.

You get out writing papers and a pen to write questions and answers instead of sitting down together at a table to talk openly about the case and your upcoming appeal. The old cell house had areas available where prisoners and lawyers could be watched through a window and were able to discuss the case, trusting no one was taping and overhearing the conversation. The lawyer tells the prisoner they have lined up an expert witness, but can't do proper tests over a phone and through windows with glass and steel bars.

The prisoner is into post conviction in his appeal, the last most important step before going into federal court, yet the lawyer's hands are tied because of being unable to fully represent the prisoner through a glass and steel bars, and over a phone. The DOC [Department of Corrections] doesn't want the prisoner to be represented as he should be and has a constitutional right to be. They're saying, 'To hell with him and his rights; we're running this show.'

It's impossible to have a confidential attorney–client visit under the present conditions for DR prisoners. All know it as does the DOC, but after a year of living in a new bunker dungeon-style prison, no changes have been made. The prisoner gets discouraged at not being able to discuss the case with the lawyer and his lawyer is discouraged, too. They lay down the phone and stand up to stretch for a minute. Fortunately, this prisoner is able to read and write. There are those prisoners who can't do either, making a bad situation even worse.

They sit down again to try to get said what needs to be said, even if it has to be written out. The prisoner is ready to leave the lawyer, who has to see another prisoner on Death Row. Some lawyers have up to a half-dozen clients they are trying to represent on their appeals. It is a constant battle and the state has claimed two prisoners this year in less than a four-day time period. The prisoner pushes the button on the intercom. The control room guard pops the door. The prisoner waves good-bye to the lawyer and heads toward the cell, discouraged, disappointed, knowing things aren't any better than before.

You get back to the cell in time for late cold chow. Beans and greens, toilet food. Feed charlie, it'll eat anything. You ask a guard about your 15-minute weekly call. But, nobody is home or you get the answering machine. The afternoon passes and you spend some time on the floor, stretching and doing basic floor exercises. You write a letter home or to the lawyer, spend an hour or so doing hobby craft painting, drawing, building something with sticks.

4 p.m.: Shift change. Time to count and pass out the mail. A guard looks in the cell but keeps going like he's being chased or something. No mail today. It's like that sometimes. Run men pass out ice once a day. Kool-Aid comes on the same cart the milk and coffee came on. Very few prisoners chance drinking the Kool-Aid. Its taste is terrible. A little later, the chow box is brought onto the quad and guards pass out trays. The last dozen trays' food is so cold, it's inedible.

You catch the local and national news on TV. No cases are discussed. Trays are picked up by run men and you are locked down again for it's shower night. You get three showers a week, 15 minutes each one. You come out of the cell and carry your trash sack to the dump. Taking a towel, soap and shampoo, you get locked in the shower. If finished before the time limit, you hit the intercom (yes, even in the shower) and the control room opens the shower door. Pick up your trash sack and head on back to the cell.

It really has been a rare day for seldom do you get to visit with loved ones and your lawyer in the same day. Anyway, you get the laundry bag ready to send out and run men pick it up. Your bean hole shuts and you're isolated again until the next day except for count times when a guard shines a flashlight in your eyes to try to get movement, see if you're still alive or see you breathe. You read awhile, watch a TV program and get ready to hit the concrete rack.

Events of the day pass through your mind. It's just been another day in the most restricted prison in the nation for another prisoner on Death Row. This is roughly just a description of one day in the life of one on Death Row, leaving out any mention of the hatred, loneliness or the fear that exists in some. Neglect and abuse of constitutional rights is a very real problem faced seven days a week. Yes, it may well be the highest ultra max security prison in the US, but at the same time, civil rights are being trampled and stomped upon, laughed at by those in authority over men who are literally fighting for life.

H-Unit. Yeah, boy, H is for Hell. Capital H. Just another day on Death Row behind the walls of McAlester, Oklahoma.

Anthony J. Mann, Death Row,
Oklahoma State Penitentiary, McAlester

Held by the Walls

Who is encased beyond the Walls
  It is I
Who sits on the Row
Waiting for Life's end, beyond the Walls
  It is I
Who weeps on the inside
For a beautiful child, beyond the Walls
  It is I
Who was unjustly tried
And now I stands, beyond the Walls
  It is I
For whom my heart aches
Mother is dead, I am beyond the Walls
  It is I
It's not beyond belief
It is I, beyond the Walls
It is my heart

As I look back, beyond the Walls
A bent knee and a bowed back
A solemn wave sending no Love, good bye
I am waiting
For I am, beyond the Walls.

John K. Barefield, Death Row, Huntsville, Texas

The Land Lord

Feeling a beckoning wind blow thru
The chambers of my soul I knew
It was time I entered in
I climbed within and stared about –
I was home indeed my very seed
A mirror of me reflecting myself
From every curve and line and shelf
Every surface there   Every texture bare
Every color tone and value   Each sound
Pride   Hate   Vanity
Sloth   Waste   Insanity   Lust   Envy   Want
Ignorance black and green
I felt myself at every turning
Set my very mind to burning
Face to face no way to dodge
Headlong I tumbled thru this lodge
I felt and met alone myself
A red scream rushed forth   But I caught
it back and checked its force
It crescendoed into a hopeless heavy weight
in the blood and fell ...
A beat of wing I felt and heard
Not at all like any bird
Overhead I saw myself contorted black
and brown and twisted mean – borne aloft
by a gray bat wing – growing from
my shoulders there ...

One thing was peculiar clear
There was no scorn to menace here
This is just the way it is
Laid bare to the bone
And I built this house   I alone
I am the Land Lord here

Gary Gilmore

Gary Gilmore was executed by hanging at Utah in 1977.

Life on the inside

Jail is a world of strife and hate,
Inside these walls you trust in fate.
Your life is run by the warden's nod
There is no peace, there is no God.
You do your best to try and cope,
To keep your spirit and not lose hope.
It's an endless struggle on the human brain,
To keep your mind from going insane.
You fight each day just to make it through
To a brand new day with nothing to do.
The one and only golden rule
Is to fight like hell just to keep your cool.
At a word or a nod tempers can flare,
And sometimes it's sad, but you just don't care.
You feel like you're sitting on a narrow ledge,
With one false move and you're over the edge.
It marks your hand like a brand or a ring:
For the rest of your life you can feel its sting.
It's like being cut, like the slice of a knife –
Living in jail is a whole different life.

But no matter how they kick you around,
You can never, never let them see you down.

Daniel L. Crispell, Death Row

Complaints on Death Row

Housing for Death Row inmates varies from state to state. Since I'm housed in the state of Mississippi, I'll speak primarily from daily life here, acknowledging conditions will make daily life better in some states and worse in others.

In Mississippi breakfast is brought in around 7.00 a.m., lunch around 1.00 p.m. and supper around 6.00 p.m. On weekdays, excluding holidays, each person is allowed one hour out of their room for recreation plus 10–15 minutes for a shower. There's opportunity for a personal phone call twice a week and a visit twice a month.

Many people on Death Row have many complaints. Complaints should not be seen as a lack of remorse for actions people may have committed in their past. I'd encourage people to reach for all they may reach for in life, not letting their past or disenchanting opinions from some of the public hold them down.

The law says Death Row inmates can't be detained in isolation solely because of the sentence of death, yet in most every state we are. If you've heard the term *the hole*, this is the common conditions a Death Row inmate is confined under. The law says a person cannot stay housed under these conditions for *years* without extenuating circumstances calling for it, yet this law also is ignored.

When MS Death Row inmates were moved from one housing unit to another, there was a hunger strike (proper grievance channels had been pursued without reply from the administration), by all who were physically able to strike. After three days the prison administration claimed they could not listen to inmate problems where there was a strike going on, but acknowledged that the new facility had wrinkles they would try and iron out. The administration asked for six months to try and work out problems. Inmates remained patient for this whole length of time, and still, none of the unconstitutional conditions had been corrected, and prison authorities would not reply to inmate grievances written out according to prison procedures. Still, no Death Row inmate has ever protested violently. This is commendable when approximately 20% of the Death Row inmates had been assaulted by officers by that point in time.

In another situation, I returned from an extradition to the state of Florida. I returned to hear a guard brag about jumping on one inmate, telling me I would get the same if I wrote any complaints. After a few days, I did write a complaint because I still had not been given sheets or blankets. The same officer told me my written complaint had gone in the garbage, then physically assaulted me after I told another authority what this officer told me. (The authority I told is the one who related the information to the officer who assaulted me, and gave him the go ahead to assault me.)

Far against my normal mentality, I made a cut on my thigh with a razor blade to try and get away from this unit and be held in the inmate hospital where I could at least be warm. Because the first month I was back from Florida I wasn't given any sheets or blankets, nor jacket or thermal underclothes, and my sweatshirt was taken from me for no reason (other than my charge involving a law officer and the prison personnel disliking my practice of following proper grievance procedures with complaints). Freezing night after night certainly can distort the mental process. I wrote and wrote about this problem, no one in the administration would help me. I was constantly told they had no sheets, blankets, etc. until my attorney called up a month later, at which time I was given these things on the very same day.

Furthermore, when I tried to complain about when I was physically assaulted, I was assaulted again for complaining. I've written from Internal Affairs to US Department of Justice about many people being assaulted, offering names and dates and witnesses, but no one cares to investigate.

Who really cares if a Death Row inmate is being beaten or mentally suffering well beyond what our Constitution calls cruel and unusual punishment prohibited by law? Many people care, but not the majority. If you aren't part of the majority, you're a radical leftist. The point is, *the majority* is stronger than *the law*.

Medical department? It bothers me to have to unnecessarily give up my one hour recreation after a long weekend in my room, only to see a doctor who keeps on walking while I try and explain a medical problem. They make it clear they don't care. It bothers me when an elderly black man with high blood pressure complains about pains and a nurse won't even see him. You see the doctor once a week. If you're not next to death, you will get nothing for medical problems. I've had to beg over 16 hours for an asthmatic inhaler before, listening to officers joke about 'You're dying anyway' when I asked for it.

Other problems? Many:

I complain about outdated rules against things like harmless nail clippers or simple writing pens that officials are scared inmates will too easily write the courts with. Since shower temperature can be set by guards and not by inmates, I have a problem with them being too hot to stand in till the water runs cold, then too cold to stand in. I complain about silly actions like an officer hiding and tearing up pencil sharpeners when they don't want to let an inmate sharpen their pencil, or cancelling our recreation hour indoors when it rains outside. I'm grateful for food, never forgetting less fortunate people because I have been there to some degree, but I complain about it being thrown together as if it were going to animals.

I hate to send out laundry for it to come back dirtier than it was when I sent it in. I also hate that in order to have my sheets and blankets washed, I have to sleep without them one night per week just because the guards would rather gather it together at night than in the morning. I hate my mail to be illegally censored, having cartoons, newspaper articles, religious tracts and such returned to sender – all, contrary to applicable law.

I complain about personal phone calls being for only five minutes, twice a week. With this I complain about visiting being on a Wednesday when people are at work and kids are supposed to be in school, and it only being one hour twice a month.

I can go on and on and on. There's no religious services, though people prove themselves responsible while being together at recreation, even while competing. A person can't have a watch, can't have a ring with sentimental value, there's no recreation equipment, there's no library service, we don't have law library service as we're entitled to by law. Some things can seem very little to some people, but little things can often become big when so much of the rest of the world is eliminated.

When MS Death Row went on a hunger strike for the things above, like medical needs, worshipping together, mandatory civil rights and reasonable sharing with loved ones, the media reported the hunger strike was for ice cream and VCRs. And really, they are a fair representative – sadly, they showed the public majority just what they'd want to see, that the human needs of the Death Row inmate are only a joke. And I complain about this.

Tracy A. Hansen, Death Row, Parchman, Mississippi

House of Horrors: the mentally ill on Death Row

Mellaril, Prolixin, Haldol, Stelazine, Thorazine, Navane, Trilafon, Elavil, Triavil, Desyrel, Asendin, a little Artane or Cogentin to help take away the muscle spasms these drugs induce, or to keep your tongue from swelling and filling your mouth like it did in Joe Turner's before he finally had enough and hung himself with a guard sleeping in a barber chair right in front of his cell. The names of these drugs and the body's reaction to them are things you learn well when you are introduced to the psychiatric services in the Texas Department of Corrections, especially on Death Row.

I live on an Administrative Segregation cellblock, one of two maximum security punishment wings on Texas' Death Row.

Throughout the day and night this cellblock is usually filled with long drawn out screams that echo in my head. More often than not 2 or 3 of them choose the same time to scream, relieving themselves of the pain and tension that has built up inside from the years of abuse and neglect they have received in response to their insanity. I can hear them fighting with their demons, punching the air and the walls, pounding on the security screen that covers the bars, or pulling the mattress off of the bunk and beating on the bare metal sheet underneath.

If I were not here witnessing the atrocities perpetrated by this system I could be persuaded to believe that the system is doing everything it can with a very bad situation, but I happen to know that their intent is nothing less than evil and there are methods to their madness.

The following is a verbatim account from a Death Row prisoner here that briefly experienced the other side of sanity and the 'treatment' Texas Department of Corrections gave him.

'I'm Pedro Miniel. About a month ago I hurd some very strange thing voices and these voices told me to hurt people and myself. I beat my hands against the wall, and yelled I also got naked. I didn't hurt nobody but myself a little, and I was taken to infirmary given a shot. I was then taken to Ellis 2 Unit, and put in strip management cell for about a week or so. I told these doctors I did hear voices, but my problem was a physical one not a psychological one, and then they told me about we can give you this or that drug. Like it didn't make a difference. And I asked them about after effects on this drug and they said sure every drug has side effects, but we can give you another drug for that like cogenant.

And, after I wouldn't take the drug they were upset because I wouldn't play the ginney pig role. Why in this strip management cell you have nothing no toothpaste no toothbrush not even shit paper. You have to ask for that, and they give you very little shit paper. I asked them to shave and they said no because I would kill myself. I said that's bullshit.

All they feed you while in strip management are "johnnies" cold and you do lose weight. I went from 200 pounds down to 184. I think they drug the juice or tea they give you over there.

I went to this wing with crazy people on it and was given sheets to sleep on. After I begged for a toothbrush this vato brought me one, and later I got some tooth powder, but very little. And, I did shave and gave the razor right back when thru shaving. Took showers but never given shower shoes. Also people are very crazy over there yelling all day all night. People get beat up on a daily basis. And, they pass out dope like candy, always tried to give me that shit.

I also believe a officer told me: "you take those yellow

butterfly pills and in 6 months you don't know your own name".

The only test they did take on me was a blood test, and never told me why or nothing. They came to me one day, and I said "Where am I going?" They said to take a test. I said "what kind?" The officer didn't know, but the doctor did and wouldn't tell me anything.

I went back to Ellis 2 a week later, supposedly for striking an officer, but can't remember because I did hear voices. And, right back to Ellis 2 where nothing was done. But, was given another shot here first before leaving the Unit.

This time I was beaten up a little bit, and I believe they gave me some shots, but can't prove it. That's about it, nothing done, nobody cares.'

Robert West, Death Row, Huntsville, Texas

This job is killing me ...
Just doin' my job

I'm just following ORDERS ...
I'm jus' doin' my JOB ...
Jus' do what the Warden tells me,
I'm just another workin' slob.

If Wilson says to gas these folks,
It's my job to do as I'm TOLD.
(I dunno NUTHIN' about HISTORY
World War Two? I ain't THAT old!)

Killing's on my job description,
Cyanide is the prescription ...
(Guess the BIBLE's got a prohibition ...
uh! my NAME ain't for distribution!)

I'm just a legal serial killer,
(livin' next door to YOU).
I volunteer to kill 'em all
(yeah, I love it, that part's true).

The folks I kill did what I do.
But now, THEY gotta die ...
My job's to follow orders,
NOT to question WHY.

Some pray, some cuss,
And their children fuss ...
It's a really ugly scene,
But the Warden says 'Kill',
And I drop the pill,
I don't do it to be MEAN ...

They beg or cry, or quietly die,
Their loved-ones suffer, too.
Just like the victims already gone,
It's my JOB ... it's what I do ...

Killing folks is just my job,
So leave me alone, okay?
I gotta git me some sleep, ya see,
Tomorrow's another day.

Douglas Clark, Death Row, San Quentin, California

Officers working on Death Row

As long as there are inmates on Death Row, there also will be officers; at least that's what keeps me here. It's far from professionals who fill these jobs. Officers, at least in the state of Mississippi, make little more than someone living on welfare. This, and the fact that most prisons are located far from a populated area, means the people who fill the position of prison guard are often the least qualified for the job.

To top things off, the title 'Prison Guard' is one that may attract a strange variety of people, from homosexuals with no more than a sexual interest in the position, to insecure, sadistic people seeking to reign over, and abuse other people. Still, I would say the majority of officers are everyday people who just try and do their job and go home. Many have no negative personal interest with the inmates.

I've been physically assaulted four times by officers at this institution. Twice I have been physically assaulted in the last year, as have 20% of the Death Row inmates here. Three assaults to me have been by ranking officers – a Captain, a Lieutenant and a Sergeant. This gives a very negative signal to new officers.

A big sadness to this is how it changes people. Not yet considering the inmate, a new officer often grows several negative attitudes in the first year of service. Inmates are beaten while their legs are shackled and their hands are cuffed. To watch another human being be treated like this, it is very unhealthy for anyone who watches, and of course to those who participate. The grievance system for inmates is ineffective enough to be non-existent. This further gives a go ahead to inhumane treatment to inmates.

Besides physical abuse, there's verbal abuse. Many officers spend most of their waking hours at the institution. When one officer hears another officer saying things such as 'I'll drop the gas on you myself ...', 'Write a grievance, no one gives a shit about you ...', etc., this also can negatively touch an officer mentally and emotionally.

Another fuel to this harmful fire is constant negative programming to the officer, concerning the inmates. Officers come in early to be briefed on any wrongs inmates have done, any new tricks inmates have learned against the rules, etc. This information is important to the officer. This can be a need to insure institutional and personal security, but this briefing is administered without consideration of the dehumanizing effect to the inmate. Very few inmates break rules, but all will be looked at in light of any violator. This briefing places an emphasis on the peer pressure supporting 'us against them' that reduces a person to a problem.

I feel like I have been bashing officers, but this is not how I feel. The real monster is a vicious system which continues in old, outdated, immature ways, propelled by cliques of ignorance.

I don't say officers are all beat down by ignorance and have no gentleness at heart. I have concentrated on the worst, because it needs the most attention for the pains to be overcome. Except for the very rare Death Row officer that is extremely mature in personal development, if there is such a development for such an immoral situation, a Death Row officer cannot help but to be victimized by the situation. Another sad reality calling for a breath of understanding.

Tracy A. Hansen, Death Row, Parchman, Mississippi

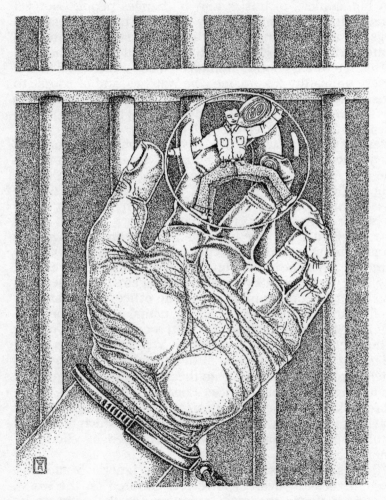

Steven King Ainsworth, Death Row, San Quentin, California

Metamorphosis –
the art of changing men to stone ...

Hearts of stone
Confined within stone
Unyielding through the day
Crumbling in the twilight.

Cracking paint
Sagging bunk
Scowling face
A fall to Grace.

Mundane routines
Pains unseen
Thunderous nights
Tedious plights.

Condemning lies
Thin family ties
A judge in black
No more going back.

Heartache and tears
Regrets and fears
No chance to atone
With a heart of stone.

Trovatore Poetaster, Death Row, Huntsville, Texas

Going ... nowhere

Packed ... ready to go –
I'm moving today, but not really.
Moving to a new place, but not really.
A change of scenery, but not really.
A new view, but not really.
　Same red brick ...
　Same cold steel bars ...
　Same cold steel bunk ...

Unshining sun – clouds that can't be seen
rain from a dreary sky, on a dreary day
Falling on a dreary place ...
Good day to move, but not really.

Echoes

Echoes reverberating between solid stone walls
Laughter, shouts, screams, down long lonely halls
Echoes within echoes, reminiscing of some distant past
Echoes of freedom that can't be grasped.

Martin A. Draughon, Death Row, Huntsville, Texas

CHILD ABUSE
AND WARNINGS TO THE YOUNG

For they starve the little frightened child
   Till it weeps both night and day:
And they scourge the weak, and flog the fool,
   And gibe the old and grey,
And some grow mad, and all grow bad,
   And none a word may say.

The old believe everything; the middle-aged suspect everything: the young know everything.

Oscar Wilde

Scars

I remember the first time my eyes really witnessed the *scars* on the bodies of almost every one of my fellow prisoners.

I was outside on a maximum custody exercise yard. I stood along a fence, praising the air that the yard gave to my lungs that my Death Row prison cell didn't. I wasn't in a rush to pick up a basketball or do anything. I just stood in my own silence.

I looked at the other prisoners on the yard playing basketball, handball, showering and talking to one another. I saw the prisoners I felt closest to, John and Pete and David, lifting weights out on the yard.

I noticed the unbelievable similarity of the whip-like scars on their bare skin, shining with sweat from pumping iron in the hot sun.

A deep sense of sadness came over me as I watched these strong and powerful men lift hundreds of pounds of weights over their heads. I looked around the yard to see if the prisoners besides John, Pete and David had the same type of scars. Sadly enough, they did. There were men on the handball and basketball courts, in the shower, and elsewhere that seemed to have whip marks and deep gashes all over their bodies. It shocked me silent to look behind their legs, on their backs, all over their ribs and see the gruesome discovery of this entire yard of men with the evidence of the violence in their lives.

Here, hidden, were America's lost children – surviving in rage and in refuge from society. Most of us were born in the fifties and sixties when there were few laws protecting us from the child abuse that victimized us.

Then, as sudden as a shock, a terrible sense of sadness came over me. I thought of my mother, who had died within that year. 'Wow', I thought, 'I still wish I had been there when she died.'

Suddenly, all of the acts of abuse that had taken place in my childhood just came to the surface. I remembered being beaten and whipped by my step-father and all the silent and lonely nights and days of abandonment by my mother, who was a heroin addict.

Only recently, in the '80s has this society come to know and realize with some understanding the alarming rate of child abuse in this country.

Yet, what is lost and given up on by society are the men who walk the prison exercise yards throughout the nation for crimes often related to the horrible violence done to them as children.

No such connection is seen by either the adult in prison who was abused as a child, or by American society at large. A prisoner will not use the term 'child abuse' as his/her own.

But because our histories were so connected, it was as if we had all had the same parents. I made up my mind that sometime that day, I would bring John and Pete and David together. I wanted to talk about the scars I had noticed and see if I could open them up to think about their abuse as children.

I was a trusted comrade to most of these men, and to a few of them I was their only family. But even so, to dare myself to go into their remembered pain and to convince them that they, like me, had been physically abused by our parents was something out of the ordinary for me.

'Am I crazy?' I wondered, to have this idea of wanting to open up these men who probably had never spoken openly of their horrible experiences of child abuse. 'None of these men will ever say that their parents have physically or sexually abused them,' I thought.

They looked hardened to the core as they stood around a weightlifting bench, proud of their bodies and the images they projected standing there.

It occurred to me, as I was approaching them, that such a posture of pride symbolized the battle wounds that they had 'made their bones' with. This is prison talk for 'prove your manhood'. Yet my own denials had at one time been similar in kind, when I had been hardened and never wanted to see my parents as the cause and source of the mental and physical scars I wore.

The difficulty in speaking with these men would be to somehow interpret the usual prison language of all of us in sharing our histories. Shucking and jiving is the usual way to talk to cover up sensitive matters with prison humor.

This was how John, a 28 year old, bulky, 6'3" tall convicted murderer, started when I asked him, while others listened, about the scars on his face: John explained that his father had loved him enough to have taught him how to fight when he was only five years old. In a sense, he said, he grew up with a loving fear of his father. He pointed out to me a very noticeable and nasty scar on his upper shoulder. He laughingly went on to say that his father had hit him with a steel rod when John tried to protect his mother from being beaten by his father.

I realized, as I should have known, that these experiences in John's childhood haunted him, as many abused memories do. His detailed accounts somehow told us what he must have really suffered as a child.

This was especially when he showed us all a gash on his back that was hidden by a tattoo of a dragon. It was a very ugly scar – like I imagined those of a slave who had been whipped.

As John directed me closer to see it, he said, 'Rub your finger down the dragon's spine.' As I did so, I felt what I thought was a thick tight string that moved nastily like a worm beneath the layer of his skin. 'DAMN, John, what in the hell happened to you!?' I asked.

John explained that when he was nine or ten his father chased him with a cord. John ran and tried to hide under a bed. He grabbed the springs under the bed and held on as his father pulled him by the legs and hit his back repeatedly with the cord until he fell unconscious and woke up later with a deep flesh wound. John, again with a cold smile on his face, admitted jokingly that that was the last time he ever ran from his father.

I first met John when we were both in youth homes in Southern California. We were only eleven years old. Throughout the years we travelled together through the juvenile systems until the penitentiary became our final stop.

David and Pete told very similar stories of beatings which occurred at early ages. All of their stories of how they had been abused as children spoke of a life that had a very telling side of how we all came to be in one of the worst prisons in the country.

It scares me to realize that some prisoners will eventually

re-enter society and father children and repeat on their own children what has happened to them. With no programs in most prisons that speak to child abuse, a high percentage of the prisoners abused as children will ultimately do this. Thus the cycle of abuse and crime will continue.

I believe that institutionalization is a kind of refuge for many of the men from the devastation of child abuse in their lives. Most children who were abused as children were taken from the custody of their natural parents at very early ages. The authority figures placed them in foster homes, youth homes or juvenile halls to protect the children from further abuse. These settings in most cases were adopted by the children, becoming their protective shield that kept them safe. For most prisoners abused as children, prisons are a continuation of this same process of living in a state of painful refuge.

Not until I read a series of books on adults who had been abused as children, and about healing the shame that binds persons to their past, did I truly become committed to the self-examination of my own childhood abuse. I began to unfold and unravel all the hidden causes behind why I just expected to go from one youth institution to the next. I really never tried to stay out of these places and neither did my friends.

I spoke to John and Pete and David very openly about my parents physically and mentally abusing me. I told how I had been neglected and abandoned by them when I was only five years old. I shared some of the horrors of my past – telling how my mother had left me and my sisters alone for days with our new born twin brother and sister when I was only four years old. The baby boy died from a crib death which I always believed was my own fault, since I had been made responsible for him. I spoke to them of the pain and hurt that I carried through more than a dozen institutions I had been in. And I told how it was that all of these events ultimately entrapped me in a cycle of lashing out against everything. I never wanted to look inward to face the fact that I was hurting – crying out for help long after the abuse, neglect and abandonment by my parents.

Hearing me express my own pain and hurt, they all seemed to avoid linking my experiences with theirs. The term 'abuse' spoke of a hidden truth: we had all been victims of child abuse. This was something that hurt them to agree with, and sadly, they never did.

Instead, we all just fell silent around the weightlifting bench as each one of us squatted down and thought ... We all stared across the yard at the other men exercising. The feeling I had was that we were all looking and seeing something that was clear and sad to us all.

John and I spoke again privately later that day, walking together along the fence. Surprisingly, he said to me, 'You know something, the day I got used to getting beaten up by my father and by counsellors in all those group homes was the day that I knew nothing would ever hurt me again. Everything that I thought could hurt me, I saw as a game. I had nothing to lose and just about everything to gain. A prison cell to me is something that will always be here for me.'

I looked at John as he said all this to me, and I didn't know what to say. Then it occurred to me that John was speaking for most of the men I had met in prison ... Secretly, we all like it here. This place welcomes a man who is full of rage and violence. Here, he is not abnormal, not different. Here, his rage is nothing new. Prison lifestyle is an extension of his inner life.

'Look around', I told him. 'Look at all these men. Don't we all say that we are men out here on this exercise yard? This prison defines us as such. But there would be much greater power in what you and I can see out here if we could all see ourselves as human beings first. I bet if you truly thought of yourself as one human being, and of me as another, and others out here as more human beings, you would gradually begin to wonder freely and openly about the nature of your life. Try to replace your false manhood impressions', I said to John, 'with your human existence and all those old experiences you had as a child will seek to come out. Human beings cry,' I said to John, 'and don't be surprised that you will cry when confronting your past with your human love.'

Jarvis Masters, Death Row,
San Quentin, California

Life is what it seems

A summer day at the playground
And children having fun.
From a burst of strength, or was it a moment of
    weakness,
An unfair name was thrown at one;
The victim laughs to hide the pain,
Acting as though, within was a gain,
Trying to act cheerful, still a part of the gang,
But the wounded heart, no longer sings as it sang.
Time elapses, understanding collapses,
And the gentle world appears to be rough.
There's a need to escape, as the wound grows agape,
And it's no longer so easy to be tough.
Returning home is slow, the head is hung low,
Walking alone, seems to bring the only peace.
So the dying smile lies, along with downcast eyes,
And the growing of fading, seems it will never cease.

Oh my, how life sometimes seems.
Tears, fears, and way too many years.

And the culprit of the words, who put the victim to
    the test,
Does he smile more than others, or more easily rest?
The culprit is a victim, living hurt of his own.
He has reached out and touched, by what within he
    has grown;
Pain. Pain. Pain.
And the world is the culprit, of the victim is he,
In the heart is the answer,
Only when open, can it see.

Oh my, how life sometimes seems.
Tears, fears, and way too many years.

Let's open the heart so we can find what's to see,
Like when living as one, together we can be.
The child is a symbol of what lives within us all,

And words can be swords, to make us all fall.
But it's not only what we say, nor only what we do,
That affects the relations, between me and you.
Age five can be fifty, and sixty can be nine,
And when we leave others, ourselves are left behind.
The culprits and victims are one and the same,
We each must be the other, to win at life's game.
Tear on the pillow may sometimes be.
Laughter in the air is sometimes free.
But life a success, cannot be us against thee.
All the heart without, is the heart within.
Hand in hand, the stranger is friend.
Only in love, can we ever begin.

Oh my, how life sometimes seems.
Smiles, laughter, and happiness dreams.

Tracy A. Hansen, Death Row, Parchman, Mississippi

The reality of Death Row for a juvenile

I am often asked, 'What is it like to live on Death Row?'
Considering I have been confined on Death Row in Texas for
the past 9 years one would naturally assume I could answer
the question without any problems. But to formulate an
answer poses great difficulty for me, perhaps because the
ordeal of being caged away on Death Row for many years is
a very abnormal experience.

When I arrived on Death Row at the age of seventeen I
needed only a few minutes to realize I had crossed over into,
and was trapped in, a foreign land. To say the least, a whole
new world for me, a world full of strange customs, where the
natives spoke an odd dialect; a world where codes are
unwritten, passed on by elders or learned through experience;
a world where humans are dehumanized, dreams are
shattered, and the individuality and spirits of those of us held
captive here are systematically institutionalized; a world full
of theatrical characters, merely existing in pain and confusion.

After observing my new habitat for a while, and getting to

know some of my fellow prisoners, it became clear that there were all kinds of people here. While most of us come from different walks of life, the overwhelming majority are minorities, born and raised in poverty-stricken slums, filled with decay and drugs. We come from disadvantaged neighborhoods which deprived us of a quality education, and the necessary recreational programs and wholesomely structured and supervised environments and activities that all youngsters need for proper growth and development. We have been subjected to prejudice and racism at every level of society, i.e. educationally, economically, politically and socially.

The horrifying and dehumanizing conditions of Death Rows all across the US have been well documented. Surely volumes upon volumes could and perhaps should be written, revealing the agonizing pain and psychological torture we, the condemned, are forced to endure for an average of 6 to 10 years, while nervously awaiting a decision from the Appeals Courts; a decision that will determine whether some form of relief will be granted, or whether we will be murdered by the state in the death chamber, in the wee hours of the morning, under the 'thin guise of justice'.

The prison guards assigned to work on Death Row here in Texas receive no special training. And most of the guards are extremely insensitive toward those of us on Death Row, who they somehow perceive as being 'less human' than themselves. It is not infrequent that the guards go out of their way to insult, degrade and humiliate us. For example, before we are allowed to leave our cell for any reason, we are made to remove *all* clothing articles and we must stand in front of the guards (male and female), and we are told to 'run your fingers through your hair; open your mouth and lift your tongue; raise up your nuts; put your arms up in the air; turn around and bend over and spread open your butt; lift up your feet.' After we have gone through this degrading ritual, sometimes performed under the watchful eyes of guards with 'homosexual tendencies', we are allowed to get dressed before we are handcuffed and escorted from our cells to the visiting room, day room, or the hospital.

I realize our country is facing an unbelievable rise in violent crimes. In no way do I, nor any sane person I know, advocate that society allow convicted violent offenders to escape punishment. But 'killing the killers' does nothing to treat the true causes of violent crimes (poverty, drugs, unemployment, easy access to guns and other destructive devices, just to name a few). No, killing citizens convicted of capital crimes is simply an empty ritual with a high price in both morals and dollars – with no proven benefit. Think about it ...

With over 2,400 men, women and children on Death Rows scattered across 34 states in the United States, isn't it time we took a hard look at the use, excuse me, correct that, the 'misuse' of capital punishment!?

Gary T. Graham, Death Row, Huntsville, Texas

Gary Graham is a juvenile offender who has so far been saved from execution by an international campaign on his behalf.

From Death Row
Parchman, Mississippi, 1990

It sure do help to get a letter in the place.
I didn't ever had a chance to go to school
because my mother put me institution.
When I was eight years old.
When I was there people kept me lock up all the times.

They never did try to help me any kind ways.
They throw me away when I little.
My daddy is death.
My mother is still live.
I don't mean anything to them.
My daddy use to beat me up all the times.
He did for no reason.
They didn't care about. I don't know why.
I guess because that this is way life is.
I have been here about nine years.

That is way too long for anybobby to be lock up.
These people here don't care about nobobby.

My first lawyer told me they were going to kill me
and write a book about whole life.
He said I had five years to live
Then they were going to kill me.
He told me I shouldn't every been born
because he said I wasn't worth anything.
That is the sorriest lawyer I ever had in my life time.

*For the above poem Sam Reese Sheppard adapted a prisoner's
letter from Death Row, Mississippi.*

How the abused becomes the abuser

As you read this, please know that I'm not looking for
sympathy, nor do I offer my childhood as an excuse for my
crimes. I do feel however that if someone would have cared
at some point in my life, that I wouldn't be here.

I am a 24 year old white male, my name is Mark Schwab. I
was sentenced to death in July 1992 at the age of 23.
Currently, I am being housed at the newly built Death Row
facility at Union Correctional Institution in Raiford, Florida.

For the first eleven years of my life, I lived with my parents
and older brother on a small dairy farm in north-eastern Ohio.

When I reached the age of eight, my life started falling to
pieces. My parents started having marital difficulties and my
father became very abusive, not only to me, but to my mom
as well. I watched as my father physically beat up my mom
almost daily.

There were numerous times when I would try, unsuc-
cessfully, to get my dad to stop beating my mom. I would
jump on his back and try to pull him off of her, but at eight
years of age, my sixty pound body was no match for my
father's two hundred and fifty pound body. He would throw
me off of him with ease, sometimes throwing me into walls,
doors or furniture.

Once when I went with my mom to pick up my father from

the airport, my father got off the plane with another woman who proceeded to attack my mom. I could do nothing but helplessly watch. Soon after that incident, my mom went to confront my dad at the other woman's home. My brother and I went with my mother. The woman went crazy and came out of the house with a gun, pointing it at all of us. That woman is now my step-mother.

From the age of eight until almost age ten, my father sexually molested me. It started out as a 'game' in my father's own words, but it soon became brutal. He would hold me down, strip me naked and then pull and squeeze my private area. Occasionally he would anally penetrate me with either his finger or an object.

To silence my screams of pain, or my screaming begging him to stop, he would put a pillow or blanket over my face, and hold it there so I couldn't hardly breathe. Then of course, I was silent, because I didn't have the oxygen to scream with.

That sexual maltreatment ceased after I was severely burned in a gasoline fire. I was burned only on my legs, but the burns were of the worst type. The problem came when my father started beating me on the fresh, unhealed burns. Today, I have no feeling in several areas of my legs where between the fire and my father, the nerves were destroyed.

Well into the age of ten, I longed for a father's love and acceptance. My best friend's father, Robert, became my big buddy. He would play catch with me and he included me in everything he did with his own son. He did not know I was being abused, but he paid attention to me because he knew my own father did not.

One day when I was alone, playing outside, Robert approached me and said there was a new litter of puppies in the cornfield and asked if I would help him gather them so they would not die. I eagerly told him I would.

As we neared the middle of the field, I asked Robert where the puppies were because I didn't see or hear them. Robert coldly told me there were no puppies and as I turned around, to my horror, he was holding a handgun to my chest. He made me take off my clothes, he brutally molested me and raped me. When he finished, he pushed the barrel of the pistol to the roof of my mouth and he told me if I ever said anything to anyone he would kill me and my family. I was so fearful that I didn't tell anyone for many, many years. Instead, I tried to take care of my own injuries, walk as normal as possible and I burned the bloodstained underwear that I was wearing that day.

My parents divorced when I was eleven, and my mom and I moved to Florida. Though I seemed to be the pawn in their divorce, the biggest part of the abuse and maltreatment was over. Unfortunately, the damage was already done.

When I started puberty around age thirteen I developed an extreme mistrust of men. I was very confused about my sexual orientation because I had only seemed to attract other males. I became easily intimidated, ashamed, fearful, a loner, and was very confused about many aspects of life.

I will probably never understand why, but in 1987, at the age of eighteen, I sexually molested a thirteen year old boy. In early 1988 I pleaded guilty to the crime and disclosed to the judge most of what happened to me as a child. I begged him to help me with my problems, sexual and otherwise. I never, ever, wanted to hurt anyone else.

In March 1988, I was sentenced to eight years in prison as a mentally disordered sex offender, and *court ordered* to get help and counselling in a treatment program. But I never got that help. Shortly after I entered prison, the treatment program was dropped. I served nearly four years in prison and was released March 4, 1991. On April 21, 1991 I was arrested for first degree murder, sexual battery and kidnapping. The victim was an eleven year old boy. I was convicted of all charges on May 22, 1992.

During the penalty phase of my trial, which determined whether I lived or died, three psychologists testified on my behalf. One said, 'At no time during his stay in prison did Schwab ever receive any treatment at all for sex offenders, though he was likely to be a good candidate and to benefit greatly from the program with a probable successful outcome.'

Because I am under a sentence of death, obviously the sentencing judge rejected all of my problems as a reason to spare my life, even when the abuse, both physical, sexual and emotional, was proven through witness testimony.

It seems that now, just about everyone cares ... they care about strapping me in the electric chair and putting me to death. I have to wonder why these people didn't care when I was being beaten and molested, and why they didn't help me when I begged for help in 1988 after sexually assaulting that thirteen year old boy. You would have thought that the sexual assault committed by me at age 18 would have been the only reason needed to give me all the help I needed.

Instead, the state will spend around three million dollars to kill me, when they could have spent just a small fraction of that to help me, and restore me to a psychologically healthy person.

Today, my mother lives in Florida and we are very close. She visits me and we write to each other frequently.

My father still lives in Ohio on the now fairly large dairy farm and is also an accountant at a chemical plant. I tried to file rape charges against him one year ago but was never acknowledged by the Ohio authorities. My father and I do not speak to each other, nor do my step-mother and I.

Robert committed suicide in 1991 after being charged with raping and molesting more than thirty young boys.

As for me, my appeal is in the early stages, and my grounds for appeal are favorable in my opinion. Recently I started a self-study sex offender treatment program. Since no one else would help me, I am doing my best to help myself. It is my goal that if or when the state executes me, I will go to heaven with a clean bill of psychological health.

Mark D. Schwab, Death Row, Raiford, Florida

Twelve years later

I wanted to kill it
when it violated
my trust, my body, my mind, my life,
no matter that it was not a 'killing offense'.

I wanted it dead
as dead as my hopes and dreams seemed
after that night,
despite the opinion of the police

I wanted it to suffer,
like I had at its hand, the certainty of death,
premature death, by someone else's hand,
regardless of its reasons for its crime.

I wanted it in its grave
so it could never,
ever, hurt anyone again,
I didn't want to forgive, or try to understand.

Now I can remember through the pain
that it was once my friend,
and 'it' became 'him'
and he became a person again

It took a long time, this remembering;
the healing is still incomplete,
the loss of innocence, of belief in friendship,
still affects how I live my life.

But, although I do not understand
why friendship turned to violence that night,
I wonder what kind of person I would be now
if I had gotten my wish twelve years ago,
and I am thankful that I did not.

Anonymous, Death Row, Arizona State Prison, Florence

How to beat the system

If I remember right, at 2.30 a.m. I used to be sleeping, or at least looking for a place to sleep. Sometimes stepping out into life without a sense of direction just don't go the way our strange desires would like it to, as it didn't with me.

But now, at 2.30 a.m., I don't have to worry about finding a place to sleep because here on Death Row the police take care of that. Right now it's breakfast time and the only worry I have is making it through another day.

When I was 13 years old the courts started sending me to these detention centers, and while I was there they told me a whole lot of stuff I didn't want to hear, didn't want to hear because I knew better. Know what I mean? Just about everybody was covering up my crimes with a whole bunch of excuses, but with me it was just fun, at least that's how it started. Then I got locked up with people that needed crime to survive, and some that needed it to get attention. But none of that really matters does it? Once we're in, we're in, right? Wrong!

My day starts at 2.30 a.m. in this 5' by 9' cell. Across the bars they have put up some thick chicken wire so I can't throw anything on anybody. At least that's what they said it was for, to me it's just something to keep me from looking them in the eye when they come by. Makes it real hard to see the TV too.

After our small, tasteless breakfast, nothing happens till 8 a.m. Can't really listen to the radio because the police play games with the antenna. Now if ya like listening to loud church services at 3 a.m. everything's cool, Jesus stations come in real clear. Since I like acid rock I'm in trouble, I'm not allowed to do what I want anymore.

On this prearranged schedule we are forced to follow, we go outside first. This means regardless of weather conditions, cold and rain included, we have three hours to play basketball or sit around and look stupid. We used to have rubber horse shoes, and a volley ball net, but they were destroyed in an attempt to get at the police. The horse shoe stakes were bent down in the ground because somebody was about to get thrown down on top of one of them. Instead, he got choked and stabbed in the middle of the yard. I watched.

Before I start detailing the perverse acts of hatred that go on in here, I want you to know that I'm not talking for the system, I'm talking against, and about, what the system does to us without telling us why. I also want you to know that if you're going to come out of there on the right foot, you're going to have to make some decisions on your own. The system doesn't care, matter of fact they would love to have you. The choice is yours, and if you'll only slow the cool act down for a moment, you'll realize that you do have the tools it takes to beat the system. What I'm suggesting doesn't have nothing to do with waiting for 5 years to pass, because if you let your youth slip away in these centers, you'll probably end up in the cell next to me, accompanying me in my/our wait for death.

Right now you're thinking, 'What are you Mad Dog crazy?! I'll never wind up on Death Row.' Saying that reminds me of me when I was going in and out of the centers, listening to the staff put me down and falling deeper and deeper into their trap. It finally took me two trips to prison and this death sentence to realize I did what they wanted. I stopped caring about myself.

You have to understand that you have the potential to do anything you want. You are somebody, regardless of what any of those jealous people tell you. All they want to do is keep you on the bottom with them.

One of the worst things they did to me was allow me to think education was for the do-gooders. Actually, education is the ONLY road to success, so while I fought against it they laughed. I lost.

In the summer of '84, what I already thought was a bad place took a turn for the worse. There had been quite a few stabbings and bombings happening here on Death Row. We were killing each other because we let the police put bad jackets on innocent people. The police figured that as long as they could keep us fighting amongst ourselves, we would never have the time to arm ourselves with education, or do battle with the system. After a few stabbings the system let the news media start calling us animals, the public responded with their usual alarm, then the police came shaking us down for weapons. This is called creating a situation then putting an end to it so the police can say they have everything under control. They make fools out of us because we are divided and stupid. By doing that they are also getting a little more money for security purposes, but we know that's not what it's always used for.

During the shake down they tore up our personal property, including photos of our families, any crafts or hobbies we might have been passing the time with, books and legal papers. Of course some of us were mad enough to fight, and fight we did. Although I wasn't alone, I speak of my own battles that followed. Listen close because what may sound cool was nothing but a losing situation for me, as it always is when we practice violence instead of using our minds.

Upon returning to my cell, I found what little property I was allowed to have had been senselessly destroyed and the entire cell was trashed. Instead of salvaging what I could, I kicked the sink and toilet off the wall and went to throwing chunks of porcelain at the police. Just when I thought I was going to get even, they approached my cell wearing flak jackets and helmets, carrying shields, clubs and a shock gun. For the moment, and as is always the case, they had won because I was out-numbered and out-weaponed.

I was handcuffed behind my back and led to solitary where I ended up staying for 45 days. In solitary we were allowed nothing except for writing material and a pair of boxer shorts. Nothing to smoke, warm water to drink and what they gave us to eat, which was very little.

In early October I was moved from solitary back to the cellblock. From there things settled down (football season ya know?) then went crazy again after the Superbowl.

The second major shake down happened at the end of January, and once again they tore our property to pieces. This time we resorted to the largest uprising in Texas Death Row history. (Which doesn't say much for the rebels here before us.) From our cells we pulled 4 TVs off of the wall, set the barber chair on fire, broke out all of the windows, flooded all three tiers, and set enough fires to half choke everybody on the smoke. Several officers were assaulted with human waste as our cells riot lasted for 18 hours.

When it was time to move I was picked up by the shackles, cuffs, hair and throat, then used as a battering ram from my cell to the day room. All of this time, and until the end, my toes and fingers were bent as well as twisted.

In the day room I was slammed face first on the floor, a knee was mashed on the back of my head, in the small of my back and across my ankles. At that time nurse M— examined me, although she couldn't see much of me on the bottom of the pile. Without even touching me she gave the word that I was 'OK' and the beating could continue. From the day room I was carried by the cuffs, hair, throat, toes and fingers, to a gurney that waited in the outside main hall. This was for all of the population inmates to see so they could be scared by the violence. It worked because they all stepped far to the side, allowing the beating to continue. Nobody gave a damn about the excessive use of force being displayed because 1) It wasn't happening to them. Yet. 2) The system had done taken the care and concern out of their battered emotions.

The people in this prison are nothing but shells of what they used to be. You are in part one of this inner death right now. The detention centers are where these seeds are planted, but their growth is up to you.

As I went down the hall on the gurney, the toes and fingers were still twisted. My feet were bent up to the back of my head while my hair was pulled and my throat was squeezed.

In front of the solitary wing I was lifted by the shackles, cuffs, hair, throat, fingers and toes, then used as a battering ram all the way to the end of the second tier. In the cell I was slammed to the floor and piled on again, getting punched and kicked while the cuffs and shackles were beat back off. After a few more moments of beating my shorts were ripped off, and to nobody's surprise they were full of shit. They laughed, giggled and humiliated me as they ran out of the cell one at a time, leaving me full of cuts, bumps, bruises and fractured joints.

Two years later my joints still aren't the same, but that's probably because I've had my butt kicked twice since then.

On top of that physical abuse they play head games, like what you're probably experiencing now but don't really understand, as far as their long term effects are concerned. Their best game is allowing you to think you're worthless and even going so far as to make you believe it, instead of showing you that you're not.

You do have options. You can get away from this criminal bullshit and make a life for yourself through positive means, or you can keep giving the system a reason to exist by reserving a cell next to mine. There's more than enough ass-kicking and humiliating to go around.

Now if you really want to beat the system, you'll do more damage by staying out of it than you can ever do in it. It all comes down to YOU. YOU can either scream and cry about how bad you have it, which is really nothing but a sign of weakness and stupidity, or you can reach inside of yourself, grab those precious dreams and make them come true. YOU must first realize what YOU want to be, what YOU want to do. Your reach is limitless because you possess something they cannot steal. Youth, strength, and a mind that thinks for YOU.

Well, I do have things to do. I'm trying to finish a book I started so I can call myself a writer. When I'm writing in it I can't help but wonder where I might be if I would have started writing the first time I was put in a detention center. Or if I would have asked one of my teachers for directions into a career, and trusted somebody for a change instead of stealing that too.

Guess this is just what happens when ya sit back and watch life go by, instead of getting involved in it.

There is nothing but pain in here. Do you want some?

Robert West, Death Row, Huntsville, Texas

Hear the forgotten feeling

Cough, choke and die.
But don't cry out;
For the ones who want to hear your cries
Are echoing sounds in hollow hearts.

The little boys and little girls,
Not yet knowing,
Surely not understanding.
Will they grow to learn?

We all learn something,
But how many teachers
Understand nothing.

Moon to sun,
And body to mind ...
The heart,
Being left behind.

Everywhere and nowhere.

Cough, choke and die.
But do not cry out.
Just cry,
And cry and cry.

Hear for yourself
For those who will never learn to hear.

Tracy A. Hansen, Death Row, Parchman, Mississippi

With midnight always in one's heart,
  And twilight in one's cell,
We turn the crank, or tear the rope,
  Each in his separate Hell,
And the silence is more awful far
  Than the sound of a brazen bell ...

With bars they blur the gracious moon,
  And blind the goodly sun;
And they do well to hide their Hell,
  For in it things are done
That Son of God nor son of Man
  Ever should look upon!

Oscar Wilde

In the night

There is no night as dark
as the darkness in this cage.
No silence is as heavy
as this mute, impotent rage.

No figure seems as lonely
as the image of a forgotten man.
Nothing is as cold
as the touch of an empty hand.

Lifeless, though alive,
he stares out at the night,
recalling days when he walked
beneath the clear sunlight.

Gazing out at the world,
there is a stillness in his eyes;
it is a stare of desolation –
no one hears how he cries.

Soon it will be over,
the silence will be complete –
for he shall answer one last call,
bowing down before defeat.

The only regret he will have
is that no one knew he stared;
for in the darkness of the cage
no one knew how much he cared.

Stephen Wayne Anderson, Death Row,
San Quentin, California

Twilight

Darkness begins to descend,
    my vision slowly grows dim,
And as blackness embraces the sky,
    the commonplace starts to look grim.
Still, I don't really notice
    the swiftly fading light –
The day isn't *really* over,
    and it isn't yet *really* night.
There's still plenty of time
    to turn around and go home ...

Isn't there?

9.00 p.m.

As my eyes adjust
    to the absence of light,
I finally realize
    home's no longer in sight.
The security that the
    daylight hours bring,
Has ended now and
    my fears start to sing.
My surroundings are strange,
    but I'm tough; I'll handle it ...

Won't I?

Midnight

I hear strange bells in the distance –
    twelve strokes toll loud and long –
Reminding me that, somehow,
    my leisurely stroll went wrong.

I'm lost; I don't know where I am!
   Or even how I got here!
I stumbled in the darkness,
   and lost all that I hold dear.
I know the night is far from over,
   but it won't last forever ...

Will it?

3.00 a.m.

The night is now so black –
   so thick – that it's suffocating,
And I wonder how I've managed
   to get this far without breaking.
No longer can I see the path,
   and I'm getting nowhere fast, it seems;
I've reached a point of just not caring,
   ready to slip into infinite dreams.
I know beyond any possible doubt,
   that there's no point to all
      this madness ...

Is there?

Dawn

It had been dark for so long
   that I couldn't believe my eyes,
When I finally saw that golden glow
   lighting up the Eastern skies.

I thought I'd never *feel* again,
   and understanding had long since gone away –
Yet by Mercy, Grace and lots of Love,
   I've made it to this point and say:

'Only through darkness, trials and tribulations
    was I made aware of strengths within,
And only when I'd hit absolute bottom
    did I see where life and truths begin.'

'Although the darkness still surrounds me,
    I've a light now to see it through –
God has answered my wailing spirit,
    and this journey I share with you.'

Baptism of dirty windows

According to Shelley, a poet is 'a nightingale who sits in darkness and sings to cheer its own solitude with sweet sounds'. It's an apt metaphor for those of us here on Death Row who try to put words together, whether to tell our own stories or to escape them; whether to understand the 'real' world, or to create a new one.

I'm not really sure of the word that describes the phenomenon – just call it a dark malignancy – but it's what a man's heart becomes after he's been here for a while. Some of us – but only a few – fight this change, but in the recesses of our minds we know the inevitable is happening, even as we deny it.

Long, boring days filled with worry and anxiety, and even longer nights. Nights of tossing restlessly between brief dreams of the past and extended nightmares of the future. Where all the time goes, I haven't a clue. I try to stay busy as much as possible; I just need something to show for the seemingly purposeless, drifting days. To go to sleep at the end of the day without being able to say that I accomplished *something*, no matter how trivial that something may seem to others, would be to chalk up another point for the other side, one for ... that demon, whatever his name is, who subtly and consistently steals the lives of those who live in and with the shadows.

Trovatore Poetaster, Death Row, Huntsville, Texas

Still and alone

Dancing sun
laughing shadows –
my soul so dry!
Her glimmering eyes
hang suspended like lamps
from the cavern roof.
Dusty, stinging wind
whips on her face.
Oh luscious spring hurry!
In the brook –
no song, no movement
just waiting.
The darkness on the path;
the silence and I
alone remain.

Carlos Santana

Carlos Santana was executed by lethal injection in Texas in 1993.

Caged

I sit here looking out into the night, and watch the lightning flicker and flash through the sky; I hear the mighty thunder roll; the rain is falling so hard it looks like a white ghostly haze; the air is cool and damp after the heat of the day; and my mind begins to move: wondering what the morning will bring. The fresh clean smell of the air tells me it's only the first spring shower and will soon pass.

My thoughts begin to turn as quickly as the spring shower, which has already gone, leaving only the damp earth and fresh smell as a sign of its passing; moving on to carry its news of the coming seasons to those with ears to hear. The coming day will be a day of planting for those with ears to hear, and again my thoughts move on.

Moving on to the moment at hand, as I sit here on this bunk of iron, surrounded by concrete walls and iron bars in a place they call prison, built by the hands of human-beings, I wonder; is it I who am caged, or those who feel the need to build such places; is it I who am caged, or those poor souls who, trapped within their fears, paid their brothers and neighbors to build such places; is it I who am locked within the cage, or is this loneliness I feel caused by being locked out of the lives of those who built the walls? Are they caged within their fears, or am I caged within the walls? And again my mind moves on.

Moving on to those who call me friend, those who have the courage to open themselves to me and share my thoughts with theirs, sharing my feelings with theirs, sharing my beliefs with theirs, sharing my love and life with theirs; and I begin to feel the peacefulness of unity we share through our lives, and a calmness falls upon my weary mind, as the calm upon the earth after the storm, and I realize it is not I who am caged at all, but those poor souls trapped within their fears of experiencing life in its true and natural form, sharing.

And once again my mind moves on; as a long lonely stream, searching for a dream, someone to walk with me as a team; as a branch on a tree, reaching to be free, from the illusions of others which surround me; as this tired troubled earth, I've been rolling since my birth, searching for some worth; as an old dusty road, I get weary from the load, of the wounds they've sowed; and as the descending dark of night, without a speck of light, my minds grows dim, and once again I look out at the night, with eyes filled to the rim, and the tears begin to fall like rain, as my heart fills with pain at the sight of the world I see, and once again I wonder, is it really me?

Shoz Dijiji, Death Row, Huntsville, Texas

Can you imagine a world as this?

Can you imagine a world,
where the stars – never shine at night,
where the moon – never gives its light?
Can you imagine a world,

where it's always dark,
where the night – never breaks to day?
Can you imagine a world,
where it's always winter – always cold,
where the warmth of Spring can never be felt?
Can you imagine a world,
where flowers – are never seen to bloom,
where trees – never bud nor blossom?
Can you imagine a world,
where butterflies – never take flight,
where birds – are never heard?
Can you imagine a world,
where rivers – never flow to the sea,
where wind – never rustles the leaves?
Can you imagine a world,
where tears – are the only moisture, to soak the ground,
where the laughter of children is a forbidden sound?
Can you imagine a world,
where wisdom – never comes with age,
for few there are, to ever grow old?
If you can imagine, a world as this,
then you know, what the world is like,
the world, for the condemned to die!

Joe Duncan, Death Row, Alabama

The Yellow Brick Road

Somewhere outside the distant window a lone cricket sings out in its private celebration of life, as the humid aroma of recent rains on hot concrete barely overcomes the stench of a hundred living souls compressed into an abyss of lost humanity.

Darkness, in its most possessive manner, slowly steals its way forth as I stand at the front of my cell. Beyond the multiple walls of cold steel bars that separate me from all else, I can bask in the simple pleasure of watching day give way to night as my own selfish celebration that I have endured – and even survived – yet another day in this artificial hell known as 'Death Row'.

This is my evening ritual – my way of paying homage to the ability to persevere, and the inner strength that comes from perseverance.

And even in this cold shadow of condemnation, I do indeed find strength. And the acceptance that the definitive measure and molding of character is not simply the ability to survive adversity – but to overcome and even manipulate the essence of adversity into a productive entity of which I find the strength to master, as if my inner will to survive is the fire that tempers the steel of adversity, molding adversity to its purpose.

I cannot see beyond this artificial hell to which I've been confined. The horizon I see is nothing more than a scattered number of lights flooding the compound grounds and dancing with glittering fire on the honed edges of razor wire that rest in stacked coils between the statuesque 'iron curtain' perimeter. The only sign of life in this world outside is a spotlight, as it lazily rakes its way across the grounds in a haphazard manner.

But even as much as they've confined and condemned my body, there remains a part of me that is rebelliously free, that no amount of steel and stone can confine and no man can condemn.

Within the inner-self of the man I am, just as within every prisoner, there's a path that leads its way off into a different horizon than that outside our window. This path is land-scaped and lined with the symbolic fruits of hope, faith, encouragement and perseverance. Stolen moments of peace-ful solitude, providing the restoration and redemption of the humanity – and even sanity – the system has raped us of.

For each of us, that most basic primal instinct compels us to strive to maintain some recognizable, progressive forward motion – refusing to succumb to the environment – finding the inner strength to keep pushing ahead one slow step at a time. And often it is a constant struggle as this imaginative path towards our personal horizon takes its twists and turns through the highest of emotional peaks to the lowest emotional valleys.

For me, I call this imaginative escape from the harsh reality of condemnation 'The Yellow Brick Road'. And a strange road it is. An odyssey towards Oz; an exodus from hell.

There's night and there's day. With symbolic night comes the uncertainty and even fear of inner darkness. The long moments and hours of uncompromised hopelessness and despair. That intense feeling that all has already been lost and the continued fight is futile. The mocking echo of silence constantly reminding me that not only must I live alone in this cold concrete tomb – but I must die alone. Long nights of lying awake staring into the dark shadows as thoughts of what was and what might have been haunt me. The demons of darkness that stealthily creep in to rob me of my most prized possessions of hope and faith and the strength of perseverance.

And then there are times that the consuming emotional darkness of my solitary cell comforts me with a warmth of misplaced security, as if this crypt represents a symbolic death itself. A sanctuary where nothing else can invade my inner being. A protective membrane that guards against the loneliness that overwhelms me, pushing me headlong into an infinite depth of despair; a hopelessness that consumes my very soul, leaving only an inner void even more material than the steel and stone that confines me.

And there is no depth of hopelessness, no depth of loneliness, no depth of emptiness that exceeds that of condemnation.

Then comes the new day, and with it mixed confusion. Darkness has again been defeated, absent of any joyous victory as the new day does little to restore the gradual erosion of those values that compel me forth.

With the new day comes the anticipation and anxiety of uncertainty. Of overwhelming helplessness born of existing within an environment of forced conformity and dependence.

But the new day brings with it a new sense of hope and there is no hope more fanatical than that which compels me to overcome. To survive.

Life of the condemned is not life at all. Rather, it is an existence somewhere between hell and who knows where. A constant state of forced limbo where the person is neither allowed to live – or die. Only exist in a virtual warehouse devoid of emotion.

But if life is defined by the mere struggle for existence and its value judged by longevity – then perhaps by cheating these disciples of death of their claim to my life I too am worthy of that unknown cricket's celebration of life. Unfortunately, the patronizing justification and comfort in that argument eludes me. Life is not defined simply by the mere struggle for existence – as we do exist. Yet through the condemnation imposed upon us by society, there is no recognition of our individuality and humanity. Thus the state of limbo between life and death.

It is not enough that our society administers its power to condemn those least able to defend against the ultimate punishment of death. 'We, the People', in a misled and demented state of moral conscientiousness, must first strip the condemned of their humanity. To recognize the condemned prisoner's humanity is to confront the reflection of our own inherent imperfection.

And so for years a death of the inner self is methodically inflicted upon the condemned prisoners, ever so gradually that it's imperceptible.

Years on end kept confined to a concrete crypt, ostracized and alienated by society.

A continuous cycle of free-falling emotions and subjection to the endless rigor of administrative conformity, until the spirit within is broken and lost, given up in sacrificial surrender.

The strength to resist is ever so very slowly eroded until compliance itself becomes a form of adoptive security. Like a dog in a cage, poked and whipped and beaten endlessly until the very soul is surrendered and all that remains is passive flesh.

But each of us do stand condemned. Each of us will confront death without exception, just as in life there are many prisons – the least of which are of steel and stone. And for each of us there is that 'Yellow Brick Road'; that escape from the reality of our condemnation. A mental path of solace and security.

The adversity we must suffer remains and continues to plague us – continues to steal from us the humanity and individuality we so desperately cling to.

But as long as we keep sight of our own 'Yellow Brick Road', we will continue to deprive our captors of the theft of our humanity and stand strong in our inner self. Not only to survive – but to overcome.

Michael Lambrix, Death Row, Raiford, Florida

Night walk

Late at night I walk the moor
beneath a full Autumn moon,
wrapped tight in heavy cloak
for winter comes soon.

My thoughts drift on whispered wind
as I stand before a gnarled tree,
shadows cast as if into my soul
touching secret parts of me.

My spirit moves across the haze
taking passage on soft fog blown;
somewhere must be a place of rest
other travelers have known.

Late at night I wander alone,
remembering each ancient sin;
my heart mourns what is lost,
what became, and what might have been.

In solitude I stroll the moor –
an image captured in moonlight;
between swampy ground and mist I walk,
finding comfort in the night.

Stephen Wayne Anderson, Death Row,
San Quentin, California

LYNCHING
IN THE
1990's
RACISM

They hanged him as a beast is hanged!
    They did not even toll
A requiem that might have brought
    Rest to his startled soul,
But hurriedly they took him out,
    And hid him in a hole.

Oscar Wilde

Being an African-American on Death Row

I am considered a trouble-maker by the system because I happen to try to educate myself and my fellow men, but even more so for attempting to educate African-Americans. For this I am also considered a racist, but who the hell isn't? African men are this nation's outlaw celebrities. It doesn't matter what other modifiers also describe our individual essences; mechanic, police officer, left-handed, Virginian, kind, gangbanger, tall; 'African man' overrides them all and makes us all, equally, desperadoes. Don't get me wrong. I know that African-American men commit a disproportionate number of America's crimes. In fact, I need to know that, since murder at the hands of another African man is the leading cause of death in my age group. Ironically, African men have more right than anyone else to run and hide when another African man heads our way. Yet we don't (most of us, anyway) because we bother to separate the few bad from the legion of good.

American society as a whole, however, tars us all with the same brush. We have become the international symbol for rape, murder, robbery and uncontrolled libido. Our faces on the news have become synonymous with anger, ignorance and poverty.

Increasingly, America seems to be painting us into two corners. In one, we are the monsters they've always said we were. In the other corner, we're fine, but all those other African men are monsters. We are anointed honorary whites, so long as we abandon every trace of our ethnicity.

African conservatives such as 'Shelby' Steele espouse individual liberation through assimilation. In one way, he is absolutely correct. It is irrefutable that if we African-Americans abandoned our culture, stopped griping and joined the melting pot, we would be better off. The catch is the very real limit to our ambition. If we play by Steele's rules; work hard, scrimp, save and study, then one day we just might become the vice president of the United States. Therein lies the rub. In this land of opportunity we can be promised riches, a degree of respect and respectability. But we know we are still barred from the highest corridors of power. It's a crippling message. How can you expect someone to dedicate his entire life training for the Olympics if all he can hope for is a silver medal?

Drug dealing and other criminal activities are the only pursuits that offer us unlimited possibilities. Since we are already vilified anyway, goes the twisted logic, at least the sky's the limit in that arena. I'm not making excuses for the African criminal; I despise him for poisoning and shooting more of my people than the cowardly Klan ever did. But we need to understand him as a human being if we're ever going to save him, or at least save his younger brother or son.

When African people mention slavery, the rest of America yawns. But our country, with its history as the home of the slave, has yet to reconcile its reputation as the land of the free. Slavery was as evil an act as ever committed by anyone on the planet. Nazis, the Khmer Rouge; that's not the sort of company Americans like to keep. It may seem like ancient history to whites, but it doesn't to Africans. Today's problems have deep roots, and until we understand the dark side of our history, our nation will never pull itself out of its current racial morass.

Finally, and curiously, some of the stereotypes that make us seem the least human, and the most animalistic, also make us seem the most male. We are famous around the world for our physical and sexual potency. And what is more at the essence of stereotypical machismo than bulging muscles and big dangling balls? Although we hate being America's villains, it's not always all bad. In America, villains have always been perversely revered.

Have you ever heard of 'The Dred Scott Case'? *Dred Scott* v. *Standford*! The plaintiff in this case was a Missouri slave whose owner had taken him to Wisconsin Territory for a time during the 1830s. After his master's death Dred Scott sued for his freedom on the grounds that he lived for many years in an area where slavery had been outlawed by the Missouri Compromise. The Supreme Court could have decided the issue on the grounds that a slave was not a citizen and therefore had no rights to sue in Federal Courts. But President James Buchanan elected in office at the time, in days just before the Inauguration, encouraged the Court to render a broader decision that would settle the slavery issue. So on March 6th, Chief Justice Roger B. Taney announced that the majority had ruled against Scott. One argument on which the Court based its decision was that Scott could not sue because he was not a citizen. Taney, in fact, argued further that no African-American slave or free could be a citizen of the United States. But the real bomb shell in the decision was the ruling that Dred Scott would not have won his case even if he had been a legal plaintiff. His residence in Wisconsin Territory established no right to freedom because Congress had no power to prohibit slavery there. The Missouri Compromise was thus declared unconstitutional. Chief Justice Roger B. Taney handed down the Dred Scott decision and it was described by Northerners that Negroes had no rights which the white man is bound to respect.

Therefore for Blacks, Negroes, Colored people and African-Americans to fool themselves into thinking that they, the descendants of former slaves, are entitled to the same rights as citizens who have knowledge of their nationality ... is not at all rational. In order to be a legal citizen you must know what your nationality is, if not then you are not entitled to human rights.

John K. Barefield , Death Row, Huntsville, Texas

Dionne

they would never notice
you who could
silence the history
taught one-sided from their books
as if
they were responsible
for us the garden of eden
the stars the sky
the sunshine night and day
the earth when fertile
the crops when good
the air breathable

Life
they would never notice
unless
we could awake from this
deep sleep the warrior
blanketed by the negro trance
trance trance trance trance
is not peace
is not charm
not the tears
which vitiate the beauty of
your face
the music of love
the bouquet of
strength
they would deny
and we start to believe
that it would be better if
we do not hear
(the anger of our fears)
see or teach
(the trail of our travails)
the truth of their history
(they would deny)
because of
these hands
browned scarred toughened
we reach out
to forgive
to love
with the tender joy that is
our history
our country
our land
our children
our entities
(to which)
we belong
alive
we could get along.

Reality check

can you hip hop to
naughty by nature
stand censored with
2 live crew
bumrush with
ice cube
or are you blacker than
professor x
krs-one
ladysmith black mambazo
do you hear
queen latifah
sun ra
what are you brothers about
nowadays
when
the fire in your heart
no longer burns
for life
but pleasure in
power
gold
white flesh
uzi determining
what slave chains could not do
how many of you know
what langston hughes was thinking
at 23 27 your age
or who paul laurence dunbar
was writing for
we the niggerati
whose skin we hate more than
our selves
we who gladly accept
the long-handled mop and pail
over that of books and brains
we sweat
to scrub away the reminisces of

ralph ellison richard wright
zora neale ahhhh! ms. hurston
who gave us
'Color Struck'
but aren't we
apt to wanna be's
we wanna be
whiter than
meaner than
crazier than
better killers than
those claiming
we are no more
than junkies cracked
on wine crime infested
unbalanced
less than man
the dark dusk
moving toward
oblivion satisfied
being nothing but
living a waste of time.

Harold L. Otey, Death Row,
Nebraska State Penitentiary, Lincoln

The emotional cruelty of Death Row

'You're a nigger on Death Row, man! Nobody gives a damn
about what you think or feel,' says a fellow prisoner. 'With all
of the crime in the news today, society just isn't prepared to
be sympathetic. So forget about writing for now, baby,' pleads
my mother. Don't write! Don't write! Don't write! thunder the
resounding echoes of voices all about.

This brings me to the first of my emotional dilemmas. I am
made to be silent when I desire to speak. Made to wear a face
of indifference while emotions of every hue rise and fall inside
of me like ocean tides. If I laugh or smile or appear to be
momentarily happy it is asked, 'How can this be? Does he not
realize where he's at and for what? What shameless display

of remorselessness!' On the contrary, neither am I allowed to show anger or frustrations; for again the cynics would say, 'So mad. So incorrigible. He's a menace to society.'

Having undergone this, I can now make more than an intelligent guess at how the boy in the bubble must have felt. Outside of his bubble, threatening diseases lurked, but outside of his bubble is where he desired to be, living normal, living free.

In my case, to be happy is potentially dangerous. Hence I am forced to live in an emotionally abridged world – an unseen bubble. And like the boy in the bubble I, too, have to take a risk by stepping out of the obscurity and illusions of Death Row and taking on a human face.

Being blanketed by obscurity and illusions gives you a feeling of being emotionally suffocated. But being physically removed from the entire world and all of the things and people you love gives you a feeling of extreme deprivation.

The cruelty of Death Row has a way of rudely ripping down the curtains of superficiality and thrusting you into the deeper recesses of reality: forcing a face to face confrontation with struggle, death and survival.

Harvey Y. Earvin, Death Row, Huntsville, Texas

Red man

Each day's the same,
Each face has a name;
I sit alone in the falling rain,
While some complain that I'm insane,
   Yet:
With whom can I walk,
With whom can I talk,
Where am I to sit,
Where do I fit?
No-one can understand,
No-one reaches out their hand;
I listen to the sounds,
The screaming and confusion,
The hate and pain of men,
Human-beings in cages;

Yet:
Where do I fit,
Where can I sit,
With whom will I talk,
With whom will I walk?
I see the guards making their rounds,
Their minds have shut out the sounds;
They count us, each and all,
Black or White, short or tall,
Brown or Red, fat or skinny,
There are so many;
They are all the same,
The only difference in number or name,
Color or size, still no-one builds ties;
The light of day slowly fades,
As the sun falls,
Still there is no peace,
Through hell's halls;
  Yet:
With whom can I talk,
Where do I fit,
With whom will I walk,
Where am I to sit?
I stand looking around,
As my heart slowly sinks to the ground;
The Black, are playing basket-ball,
Or sitting along the fence,
Talking their jive;
The White, sit in a corner rapping,
Or doing their drugs,
In search of another life;
The Brown, (Mexicans), are sitting,
In another little corner, as if,
They were in a world all their own;
  Red man,
Where will you sit,
With whom can you walk,
Where do you fit,
With whom will you talk?

Shoz Dijiji, Death Row, Huntsville, Texas

WOMEN AND DEATH ROW

I am afraid of the women ... The men I can always manage.

O crucified mother, the despot has driven a nail through thy right hand, and the tyrant through thy left.

Oscar Wilde

Lunar dreaming

i wonder what it is like
to be born a woman
in this a world of male
chaos egotistical seeking
to crush the petals of
the single rose bled
red the pain
the look in her
mirror pleads
am i pretty
my lips like pears
my skin supple fresh
my eyes the thrones of diamonds
enough to capture the
forgiveness for
being born beneath
the bane of virginity
the grunt the ahhh
the why
the powerlessness
offended by the only
wanting to be me.

Harold L. Otey, Death Row,
Nebraska State Penitentiary, Lincoln

Being a woman on Death Row

Life on Death Row is *very* different for women, and in so
many ways.

Us women are *so* restricted and the men have a lot more
privileges than we do. But that's not only with the Death Row
population. Men in general, get lesser sentences and then are
able to get out of prison much faster than women. In my
personal opinion, I think they try to make examples out of
women. But then we know I'm sure, that it's very much a

man's world! I think it's harder on women because women are more sensitive and it's especially painful when you have a child, as I do. I've missed so much of my daughter growing up and I can never get that back. She was only 7 years old when we were separated and soon she will be 15. She's going to her first prom this month (the junior prom) and it breaks my heart I can't be a part of it all.

It's just different for a woman that's a mother. I guess because she carries that child inside her for 9 long months. She feels its every move, every hiccup, and loves the child before it ever even comes into this world. I'm not saying that a woman loves her child more than a man but a woman just has a special bond, and let's face it, women spend more time with the children.

It's been especially hard for me, because I was a single parent and therefore extremely close to my daughter. Plus my family lives in another state and I only get to see them at the most four times a year. And then too, I was the only female on North Carolina's Death Row for a good while, so I really felt alone. I had no one to talk to about my feelings and fears because unless you're in this situation there's just no possible way you can relate.

You go through so many different phases, emotionally, mentally and even physically, before you ever reach an even level. And even when you've been on the Row for as many years as I have been, it doesn't get any easier. Just a simple little change can throw me in a pure state of panic. I don't adapt well at all to *any* form of change any more. And being on the Row, you are automatically isolated from the general population, and allowed *no* contact, which makes you feel alienated. I'm not even allowed to *talk* to someone just in passing, that's on population. There have been times, that I was at the prison hospital, and if someone tried talking to me, an officer would immediately jump all over them and tell them to go on the other side, or back up and that makes me feel guilty and bad, that they got in trouble for just speaking. It makes you feel like you're contagious or the like! Plus, when you're on the Row, you're always last in everything. And it's even hard to get medical attention. It's almost like they're saying to themselves, they're going to die anyways!

Right now this very minute, I'm sitting here without a lawyer, so *nothing* is being worked on, on my behalf. I'm just here, and time keeps going on and I can't do one thing about it. It's very frustrating and especially when others who have only been on the Row maybe a couple of years are further along in the appeal process than I am, and I've been here the longest of any female in this state ever.

Donna S. Cox, Death Row, North Carolina

So many times

So many times
I'd see her up
  upon that stand,
It ripped through my soul.
I'd see her sit
  with a tear in her eye,
demolished the stone in me.
So many times,
So many times ...
I'd hurt her and
bring her to a place
she wants not to be;
to break down and cry.
I see the pain inside;
it lashed at me, like
  razors oh so sharp
and shred me to ribbons;
  a million tearful parts.
So many times ...
Still many months later,
I feel that pain inside,
and I do love you Mother;
this pain shall go away,
as it seeps back down
  into my heart.
So many times,
So many times ...

Mark Robertson, Death Row, Huntsville, Texas

Standing alone

I stand looking out my window
Watching as my shattered dreams drift
Across the desert floor on the
Wings of a desert breeze.
My eyes cloud over with thoughts of my past,
How I thought love would last.

Now she is living on the other side
Of my life,
Living as I stand looking out my window
In my cell waiting for the warden to
Come and shackle me –
To lead me to my final doom.

My heart filled with anger for those who are
About to take my very life.

My mind frantic in its search for compassion
To comfort my fear.
My final choice of words ringing in my ears,
As I say goodbye to my mother.
I long to reach out and wipe the tears
From her face as she so often did when I
Was a child.

But my hands are held in place
By the steel bracelets
Pulled tight to my waist
By the chain.

All I can offer is a smile to hide my fears
And my pain,
As I tell her that things will be fine.

The warden pulls gently on my arm saying,
'It is time'.
I turn and slowly walk away,
Looking over my shoulder I see my dear
Mother standing alone in the dim light.

She is saying something I cannot hear
For my heart is beating loudly in my chest.
Fear rises upwards – slowly stealing
My breath, as each step I take brings me
Nearer to death.

I stagger slightly and someone helps me
To stand,
With a word or two said we reach
The chamber door.
Inside I step to seat myself
Upon the metal chair,
And as the restraints were put into place
I realized what it was my mother had said
To me as they led me away.
'I love you too Mom,'
I say quietly to myself as my life slips away.

Daniel W. Cook, Death Row, Arizona State Prison, Florence

I never saw a man who looked
   With such a wistful eye
Upon that little tent of blue
   Which prisoners call the sky,
And at every drifting cloud that went
   With sails of silver by.

Oscar Wilde

Going home in a dream

Being scared is a lonely thing.
Often we search for others to blame.
It's hard for some to admit
To things they know they've done wrong.
But there's times when the pressure's too much
And we panic, not knowing what to do.
We get blind to the help that's there
And search for the quickest way out.
But when the wrongs all catch up
Whipping us with sorrows and regrets
We dream of going back
And doing it all so different.
Just knowing that there's no returning ...
The circumstances or options to come ...
Make us Oh so frightened and feeling alone,
Wishing we could just run away,
Wake up and appear back home.

Martin A. Draughon, Death Row, Huntsville, Texas

Deadman's dream

One day, some day
I'll awaken from this dream

Sitting, happy
Skipping stones across a stream

Someday, sometime
My dream will start to fade

Whistling, walking
Laying in the shade

Sometime, somehow
I'll no longer need to worry

Seeing, touching
Rose leaves soft and furry

Somehow, somewhere
Fate will catch me still

Unmoving, uncaring
Buried deep beneath the hill.

Michael A. Williams, Death Row, San Quentin, California

Beyond all seasons passing

Beyond all seasons passing, I have known yesterdays.
They sleep dreaming somewhere in mind, a mind filled
with musings and wondrous scents
swept up from old vaults
or by the winds of ancient fires:
memories of you and me
when great oak trees made arch-like tunnels,
shaded tunnels with diamond slits of light.
we ran, hop-scotching, shouting bravado, 'No ghosts
    here!'
we hop-scotched, children who did not yet know
the meaning of sweat or tears.

Beyond all seasons passing, I wander this path
picking fruit from memory trees, going ever on.
You giggled at my tasting of a honeysuckle flower,
but then tasted too. We immersed our senses
within stream scents, each childhood sharp:
honeysuckle sweet scents on a warm
gentle afternoon fading into twilight as we
chased fireflies. Were they real? Were we real?
When captured, they flashed in jars,
but dawn revealed only dead bugs:
dead bugs of children's fancy.
We rushed onward across a lawn of fresh-cut grass,
a scent filling us with release. We laughed, brushing
it from our hair and wet feet. The magnificent

smell of burning leaves caught every autumn breeze,
sometimes bitter, sometimes just a hint.

Then fall became winter void: cold, desolate, dread.
Echoes of what once lived
in stark etchings of bare trees
lined a smoky grey sky;
echoes of those who once knew this life as we did,
their names carved in stone,
row on row, in a cemetery on a hill beside the path.
We read names of people long gone,
most unremembered, their memories mere
granite slices and snow-blanketed soil,
sleeping soil. Yesterdays smothered by time.

Beyond all seasons passing, we stood
holding hands, observing a storm brewing above
while we played in a city of silent stone.
Dusk drifted around us as we headed home,
but we found we were somehow lost, frightened,
calling to our parents who were gone. 'Beyond us,' I
    whispered
against your cold ear, 'in the graveyard they lie.'
But there were no ghosts there, and you hugged me tight.
Maybe it was just a dream? Or perhaps we were the
    dream?
But you laughed at that, running away, and I
chased you beyond all seasons passing.

But there were no ghosts there, my dear,
and in ash comes to mind a poem I wrote
when we were children confined to childish fancy:
a poem with silly rhyme about you and me
as around us faded strains of songs
and you died in my arms
over and over again.
We did not know that things were changing
between us or that time had chased away
even the dreams of our sleep.
We fled before the storms of endless seasons,
yesterdays smothered by time,
and stood beside the sleeping soil, beside

silent stone, reading names row on row, finding
a place to carve our own names: yours and mine,
yours and mine.

Stephen Wayne Anderson, Death Row,
San Quentin, California

Mark A. Davis, Death Row,
Raiford, Florida

I can see ...

I can see the trees swaying from side
to side, blowing freely in the wind;
pulsating, throbbing – matching the
beat of my heart.

I can see the people casually walking
beyond the rows of razor-wire fences.

There are many expressions, but none
to match the loneliness, despair and
pain I live in. Only the ones who
are, or have been, on this side of
the steel can understand my suffering.

I can see the fresh, clean rain when it
falls. Each drop seems to be in slow
motion, waiting for me to drench myself
in its cleansing fragrance. It beckons,
but the cold steel keeps me from my
lustrous baptism. Most people try
to stay out of the rain; for me it's
the only way to wash off the prison
stench – the only thing I can get that's
not controlled.

I can see the little birds making their
nests high in the corners of building
and fence. I watch them come and
go through the tiny holes in the steel
chain links.

I can see that the wind whips strong out
there sometimes, pushing and spinning
things around, but I can only watch ...
it doesn't ever blow on me or bring
that sweet smell of freedom to
cheer my soul.

I can see my somber reflection broken
up by the criss-cross strips of metal
on the window. It tells of how badly
I wish I could be blown away – lifted
up and whisked away, like a tiny piece
of paper in an almost silent whirlwind.

I can see that I *am* being blown away, but
it's not by a warm Summer breeze wrapped
in the essence of freedom. It's not
by a judge writing my name on the right

piece of paper, as I hope for. Instead,
I can see that I'm being blown away by
this corrupt, violent world that our
God-given Earth has evolved into!

Martin A. Draughon, Death Row, Huntsville, Texas

Something within

I awaken.
The birds are singing.

Thoughts are stirring.
They'll encompass my mind.

Feelings are stirring.
They'll encompass my heart:
Will they flow in peace?
Will they dance vigorously?
Will they be something I want to remember?

The sun is descending now.

Soon,
The birds will stop crying.

Tracy A. Hansen, Death Row, Parchman, Mississippi

And never a human voice comes near
  To speak a gentle word:
And the eye that watches through the door
  Is pitiless and hard:
And by all forgot, we rot and rot,
  With soul and body marred.

Oscar Wilde

Two wars 1991

No more War
On the Battlefields
Or the Execution
Chambers
It's simple
One dead Prisoner
One dead Soldier
Or
One dead Child
Are tragedies
Eternal
No amount of History
Political Rhetoric
Or Law and Order
Solutions
Justify Killing
Anyone's People
It's simple
And I am not available
For argument.

November Belford West, co-founder of Endeavor

Working against the death penalty

Death Row, wherever it exists, is purgatory. It is where the people we condemn to death suffer and where some expiate their sins. It is where human beings exist in a state of anticipation of their own pre-determined deaths. No matter the conditions, whether relatively good, bad or indifferent, Death Row is not and cannot be less than physical torture. There is no way to predict how an individual will react to Death Row. Sometimes those who appear the strongest are defeated and broken. Sometimes those who appear the weakest find amazing spiritual strength. We kill the broken and reborn alike.

Conditions on Death Row depend on the prison administration. I began working on Death Row in South Carolina,
where the administration openly opposed the death penalty.
The men on Death Row were viewed as arbitrarily chosen
victims. They, their families, friends and defence teams were
treated with kindness and understanding. By the time I
moved to Virginia, I had seen harsh conditions on Death Rows
in Texas and Oklahoma, but I was totally unprepared for what
I would find in Virginia.

It is difficult to describe the inhumanity of Mecklenburg
Correctional Center in the late '70s and early '80s. Men on
Death Row and in segregation were beaten regularly. These
beatings were done by teams of guards, suited up for combat
and carrying shields and clubs, against individual prisoners.
The beatings were relentless – even when men were beaten
to the floor, they were then kicked. When word of these
beatings began to get out and receive some criticism, the
prison started videotaping the beatings. There are hours
upon hours of these videotapes, and they defy any sense of
humanity. But perhaps the most astounding aspect of these
videotapes is the fact that the prison administration was
convinced that the tapes would prove that these beatings
were justified.

Many of the men were kept on dangerously high doses of
psychotropic drugs. I have a letter in my files from a
psychiatrist recommending experimenting with hallucin-
ogens on one of the men, because, the doctor says, the man
can be kept in his cell and his life will end soon anyway. If
the men tried to refuse the drugs, they were beaten, chained
down to their bunks, and the drugs were administered by
force. Other than beating them and barking orders at them,
the guards were not allowed to speak to the men. Rules
changed weekly or more often, but the men were not allowed
to know what the rules were until they broke them and were
punished, either by beatings or being thrown into a strip-cell.
In strip-cells they weren't allowed to have anything but a pair
of undershorts. That is – no clothing, mattress, blanket,
paper, pencil or toilet paper. They had a choice of sleeping
on the concrete floor or steel bunks. Often their water was
cut off so that they could not get a drink of water or flush

their toilets. Sometimes the men were injured when they were put in strip-cells, and naturally, whether injured or not, they often got sick, but they received no, or grossly inadequate medical treatment.

The prison administration made every attempt to totally isolate men on Death Row from all outside assistance. Lawyers and legal assistants had great difficulty getting in to see their clients and were treated so badly when they did get in that most stopped going. Because I was persistent and wouldn't go away voluntarily, I was repeatedly banned from the prison.

Once, because a newspaper article quoted a lawyer as saying my counselling of men on Death Row was invaluable, the prison said I didn't have the right to counsel my clients. Another time I was banned because I was talking to my clients about God. The prison said I wasn't a chaplain and didn't have the right to talk to my clients about religion. On the other hand, clergy who opposed the death penalty and befriended the men were banned as well.

Family members and friends were humiliated by strip and partial strip seaches (for *non*-contact visits) and sexually harassed. Often they would spend hours driving to Mecklenburg on a visiting day, only to be told that their family member or friend wouldn't be allowed to visit that day. By the time I got to Virginia, most of the men's families and friends had given up trying to visit. It was understandable. They were going through all this to talk over a phone to their loved one who was locked in a concrete and glass cage.

Even during legal visits men had to wear metal chains with padlocks in the small of their backs, were handcuffed to those chains and had to wear leg irons as well. Guards sat in the room listening to our conversations, and those conversations, which are guaranteed confidentiality by our constitution, were reported to the wardens and the attorneys general who work to overcome our legal arguments and have our clients killed. In addition, there were strict orders that no one was allowed to touch a man on Death Row. A legal visit with a lawyer, law student and me was once stopped because our client began crying, and after a few moments I couldn't stand it and put my hand on his arm.

How do normal human beings reach the point of being able to treat other human beings the way the guards and administration at Mecklenburg were treating these men? We do it through a process of transmogrification. We turn human beings into non-humans, objects, monsters. We project our fears, frustrations and dissatisfactions onto them. They become our scapegoats, the embodiment of everything that is wrong with us and our society.

Finally, the facts about the conditions at Mecklenburg were taken to court. A federal judge said that Mecklenburg was in the dark ages and declared the conditions unconstitutional. A new administration was brought in, and conditions improved.

Conditions on Death Row remain unnecessarily strict, and there is an admitted and successful effort to keep the men disorientated and divided. Death Row, itself, is tomblike. Everything is off-white concrete and steel. The predominant sounds are electronic. The ventilation is so poor even the air is deadly still. It looks and feels like a sensory deprivation chamber. In the summer it is like a combination sensory deprivation chamber and oven.

To me the worst condition the men, their families and friends endure is a complete lack of privacy. Any letter going in or coming out can be read, any phone call or visit monitored. This is extemely destructive to the family relationship. Think of all the things you discuss with your husband, father, brother, favorite cousin or best friend that you would never discuss in front of strangers. Think of years of carrying around alone all the emotions that go unshared, all the things you want to say that go unsaid, and think of the pain of those unshared emotions and unsaid words after your loved one has been killed. The families and friends of people on Death Row are truly the unacknowledged, unseen victims of the death penalty.

Several years ago there was an attempt in Virginia to get contact visits for men on Death Row – they are usual in most of the death penalty states. There was an enormous uproar. Legislators and citizens alike kept repeating the theme that 'Why should men on Death Row be allowed to hold their mothers' hands when their victims would never be able to hold anyone's hand again?' Not once did any of these people say: 'Aren't we punishing these mothers enough by killing their sons? What harm would it do to let them hold their sons' hands until we kill them?' Of course, in our use of the death penalty, we *have* to ignore the families and friends of those we condemn to death. Monsters don't have families and friends. The families and friends are uncomfortable reminders of the humanity of the people on Death Row, uncomfortable reminders that they, like us, are more than the sum of their worst acts.

The suffering of the families and friends of the condemned is so heartbreaking, if proponents and those who administer the death penalty were to let it in, it would sear their souls. There is a mother who dreams every night that she is forced to plug in the electric chair in which her son is strapped and waiting to be killed. I watched a sister beg a governer's aide for her brother's life. She had been 10 and her brother 6 when their mother ran away and their father began drinking himself into oblivion and beating them every night.

Their suffering is caused by – as I said earlier – what many people in my country view as a necessary, though perhaps regrettable, policy upon which reasonable men and women can agree. But having seen all this suffering and so much more, I am unable to see the death penalty as anything but evil.

If you are involved in killing a human being, you have to rationalize that killing. One method of doing so is to convince yourself that the killing serves some good. Once you've done that, more killing must equate with more good. Dr Grigson, a psychiatrist in Texas who has been directly responsible for putting over 200 people on Death Row and who even Supreme Court Justices refer to as 'Doctor Death', has said on national television that he views himself as a savior. The Attorney General of Virginia and those in her office who work on death cases felt that the campaign for a new trial for Joe Giarratano was a personal attack on them. They lobbied *intensely* to have Joe killed. They expressed their feeling that Joe had to be killed in order to *vindicate* them. If the death penalty is good, it doesn't matter who its victims are. Professor Ernest von den Haag argues that the good served by the death penalty far outweighs the harm of killing a few innocent people.

Many sociologists, psychologists and other scholars say the death penalty brutalizes society because it sends the message that violence solves problems and causes an imitative reaction. Living and working in a killing state, I have come to realize that brutalization is not simply a sociological abstract or theory. The death penalty first brutalizes those who are closest to it, and there it can be measured. I believe there is a dangerous atmosphere in the land when law makers and law enforcers are brutalized.

About 10 years ago I read an article by a Jewish scholar, a man who had survived one of the Nazi concentration camps. He traced the holocaust back to Hitler's reintroducing the death penalty in Germany for murder. He argued that once you get people to agree that certain individuals can be killed for certain crimes, you can expand that penalty to include any crime – real or imagined. He pointed out that although the holocaust was a crime against mankind, by the legal expansion of the death penalty in Germany during that time, the killing of criminals, the retarded, gypsies, homosexuals, Jews and Christian 'traitors' was all *legal*.

His is a warning none of us can afford to ignore.

Marie Deans

Now working with prisoners on Death Row in the state of Virginia, Marie Deans joined Murder Victims' Families for Reconciliation after her mother-in-law was murdered in 1972.

Through prison I grew

Through prison I grew raised
Visiting a dark father in denim blue
Serving time for a crime he did not commit.
I grew raised through prison
For there held my house as
I walked knocked hurt from my home
– motherless, fatherless on a clear-born day in July.

And I held long-lost in a fathomless dream
Unhearing, unseeing but in secrets of my loss ...
So the focus of my homelessness became prison.
For I was raised through the prison
That stood for my father's home, The Big House,
Full of bars and stone and the gates
Wherein, wherefrom I could pass through
The portals of heaven to hell as a child
In unknowing but soon knew ravages unknown
To visit my father.

One could smell death from the implacable walls;
One could see the tears – then knew
The stench of the Hole and the blood of
The kid gang-fucked and raped, later to kill
Turning mad rabid to rabid –
For I stand raised as my father's son
In the prison of our common loss
– for I stand raised through prison –
The dying and the dead, the vicious and pathetic,
Yet some with a way of honor in their livelihood
Through the time he served innocent of his crime.

So I grew raised from prison –
The Long Walk, the high walls, caution at the corners,
Walk slow and drink a lot of water.
For I grow and grew from the prison beyond
To now search for my sister/love's eyes and loss
With her infinite caring,
With the cry of angels through the dust of our world
At our feet and our crush in the passions of love.

S. R. Sheppard

Sam Reese Sheppard lived through the trauma of his mother's murder and then the terrorism of the death penalty threat upon his father by the state when he was seven years old. He visited a maximum-security prison for ten years to see his father, who eventually was able to prove his innocence.

Sam Sheppard now belongs to the National Coalition to Abolish the Death Penalty, Amnesty International and Murder Victims' Families for Reconciliation.

Death Row poets
(for Marie Mulvey Roberts)

To wait, to watch. Vocation
Of the prisoner and the poet.

Not those who choose not to watch,
Chess-players, crossword-puzzlers, those who
    flinch

From the blazing face of Time, and focus
On small exacting things. But the poets,

The prisoners, whose stretch is finite,
Look straight in Time's face, and see

The unrepeatable marvel of each second.
Consider these prisoners, these poets.

Consider also those who are taught not to see,
To blanket violence by conditioning;

Decent men, kind to wives, who must not know
Which of them pressed the button;

Who must learn to see the dummy, not the person;
Who must be helped, by rectal plug and catheter,

Not to smell the body's final protest.
Consider these men also. And those who give them
    their orders.

U. A. Fanthorpe, LifeLines

To be seen, to be done

If you are to be seen
Why hide
Behind curtains, robes
Order and law,
If you are so true
Why lie
To the mouths that speak
Of you,
Why bite
The hand
That's feeding you.

If you are to live with us
Why not
Protect us,
We need you now
And always,
For ever
And ever
Be good,
If you want respect
Just be
As equal as we,
What do you mean
Without we.

You came to save our madness
But madness turned you on,
We have one question
Justice,
That is,
Where have you gone??

Benjamin Zephaniah, LifeLines

Capricious and ugly: America's horrible lottery

Imagine a game where winning lets you get away with murder. Where a draw puts you in prison for a few years. And where losing leads to a grisly execution where you are cooked to death so forcefully that your eyeballs pop out and your body catches fire. Alternatively, the losers might instead be poisoned, hanged, gassed à la Auschwitz, or shot. You have a 51% chance of winning. You draw nearly 49% of the time. The chance you will lose is less than one time in one thousand. Want to play? Over 25,000 Americans play that roulette every year. About 20 to 30 lose the game. Yet all of them draw the same entry ticket: killing one or more other human beings. There is no predictable pattern indicating who will win, who will draw, and who will lose – with the minor exception that you are slightly more likely to lose, and to be cooked, if you live in the Bible Belt southland.

Other than abortion, capital punishment is America's most turbulent social issue. People debate endlessly over the state-sponsored taking of a life, for one individual's willfully taking a life of another. Opinions are strongly divided. Many feel the punishment should be swifter and more certain, executing up to the full 25,000-odd citizens who murder every year, or at least those who are caught and convicted (for about 30% are never apprehended, another 20% or so are declared not guilty). These believers note that in nations like Saudi Arabia, where criminals are convicted, sentenced, and beheaded in one day, the murder rate is almost non-existent. Others feel the more barbaric forms of execution should be changed, eliminating the electric chair and the gas chamber even as society earlier banned decapitation, strangulation by hanging, and burning at the stake. They favor killing the convicted (some of whom might not be guilty), but doing it more humanely. A possible oxymoron. Still others like the present system: place the condemned in tiny cubicles, refuse them the opportunity for work or constructive pursuits, keep them mostly indoors and isolated, then torment them for ten or fifteen years – or more – not knowing whether they will lose or draw. Drag it out in ways that stress their sanity, occasionally letting them watch other inmates be taken down the hall to their doom. That is considered 'treating them fairly'.

A minority of the US population, about 25% according to a recent survey, favors eliminating the death penalty. Out of step, as it were, with most of our population they are in step with the majority of the world. Only South Africa and Russia, among industrialized nations, continue the death penalty. China and a number of other less-well-developed countries also routinely execute their own citizens.

Since the death penalty was reinstated, less than two decades ago, there have been perhaps 300,000 felony murders in the US. That is more than all the American servicemen killed since the end of the Civil War. Deaths by murder exceed deaths from traffic accidents plus plane crashes, every year. No one knows the true figure, for many deaths ruled 'accidental' or even 'of natural causes' were actually homicides. Although many believe that the threat of capital punishment is a deterrent, the record indicates it is far from an effective preventative. Homicide rates are almost twice as high in the states that have carried out executions since capital punishment again became legal, as in the 14 states which prohibit death sentences. The overwhelming majority of murders are impulsive, or occur under such stress or mental impairment (typically, drugs or alcohol) that the killer cannot or does not reason beyond the immediate moment. Threats of potential future punishment are meaningless in such circumstances.

Most of those convicted for killing another person receive sentences of lifetime imprisonment, or some lesser number of years of incarceration. During the 1980s, only about 270 death sentences were handed down annually, on average. That number may now have risen to something over 300. Well over 90% of those sentenced to death have either been pardoned, had their sentences commuted, or remain on Death Row. About 5% have actually been put to death. Hence even those who think carefully about killing someone else may quite reasonably conclude that they are unlikely to be caught, or will avoid conviction, or will get a lesser sentence, or even if they receive a death sentence it will not be carried out.

Proponents say that by those crimes the guilty have forfeited their right to live in our society, and that we are better off without such people. This implies a once-a-murderer, always-a-murderer belief, a wish to be 'protected' from future killings. Yet abundant statistics show that released murderers virtually never kill again. Another view, often coupled with those just stated, is that victims' families 'deserve the satisfaction' of seeing the wrongdoer put to death. The argument is not for bloodthirsty reprisal, but instead that it would be 'unfair' that a killer should be permitted to walk free, or even to live, in the face of a family's irrecoverable loss. They are not bothered by the contradiction that they can be deeply grieved over one death but can be comforted by another. Nor are they bothered that friends and families of the convicted will also suffer and mourn the retributive death of their parent or child. A further variant of the argument for capital punishment is that murderers (and certain other criminals) are 'enemies' of society. That is felt especially strongly about cop-killers, traitors, and those who murder the helpless. With militaristic simplicity, they observe that the easiest way to deal with an enemy is to destroy it. Some people combine one or more of those views with a sense that murderers are flawed – that they lack a sense of caring or concern for others, or that they are heartless or even take pleasure in cruelty and death. Generally such people feel that the defects are uncorrectable. In the quest for a more perfect society, they feel such flawed citizens should be eliminated.

Dr Martin Luther King, Jr, observed that the death penalty is society's final assertion that it will not forgive: 'Men will continue to worship the god of revenge and bow before the altar of retaliation ... but only goodness can drive out evil and only love can conquer hate.' Views such as Dr King's do not condone murder, nor ignore the horrible impact it has on victim families. There is dreadful pain when a loved one, especially a child, is lost pointlessly and perhaps cruelly. Such a loss can never be compensated and is never forgotten. Yet those who teach us how to live, such as Dr King, uniformly oppose vengeance even under such extremes. Vengeance diminishes the individual and demeans the society, we are taught. The New Testament followed by Christians nullifies and vacates the old Mosaic law of 'eye for eye and tooth for tooth'. One of the primary purposes of all religion, all moral codes, and all ethical structures is to encourage people to be considerate and forgiving of others – even when they have not earned or warranted such a response.

We should recognize that failure-free law enforcement would have us apprehending, convicting, and sentencing to death over 25,000 persons per year. That is a figure higher, for example, than the number of MBAs or new lawyers graduated annually. It even exceeds the number of killings shown daily in all the TV programs and all the movies. We would be executing at least eighty people daily, except for religious observances on Sundays. Of course, each of those executed would already have killed one or more other people. One can ponder whether that rate of retributive executions would effectively display the message that wanton killing is immoral and must be stopped.

There remains a potent moral argument over whether the lottery of death should be permitted to continue. Those who are executed are only a token fraction of those guilty of murder. The threat of execution is manifestly not a deterrent to crime. Putting to death a small number of people every year is no more than symbolic satisfaction of the widespread desire to kill, in retaliation, all of those who commit murder or some other appalling crime. (And there is no evidence at all that these are the persons who 'most deserve' to die.)

That our system constitutes a lottery, instead of a consistent pattern of enforcement of justice, is clearly unfair. Possibly it is even more unfair to society at large than to the individuals who are sacrificed. As long as the death lottery exists, we will have a system that is inconsistent and capricious, thus unfair to individuals and to our society.

There are two ways to eliminate the lottery. Either execute every condemned person within 24 hours of sentencing, or abolish the death penalty. Any intermediate course, which might permit some to escape through legal procedures, delays, or clemency actions, would do nothing except further change the rules and odds of the lottery.

Under the first option, even with no improvement in the rate of apprehension, conviction, and condemnation, the rate of executing people would have to increase ten-fold just to keep even with the new sentencings. Along with that, to empty the Death Rows of accumulated prisoners, say over ten years, would require nearly a twenty-fold increase in executions. There would then be about two executions daily in the US, with Sundays taken as a holiday. Even that would accommodate only the felons actually apprehended, convicted, and sentenced to death. Responding to every killing by another killing 'in the interests of justice' would require not two executions daily, but 65 or more. Presumably a stronger commitment to carry out executions would be paralleled by a greater willingness to impose the death penalty on those convicted of capital crimes. Then we might see three, four, or even more legal killings daily – or possibly less frequent mass executions of dozens or hundreds of felons. Quite aside from how the US would then appear to other nations, it is obvious that two or more executions daily would have a numbing effect on public sensitivity. Even though the streets would not be running with blood, executions would no longer be newsworthy.

Under the second option, still more of those who 'deserve' death would not pay that penalty. But it is only a small, symbolic percentage of murderers who become victims of the lottery. One must wonder how severely the public interest would be harmed if those 20 or 30 persons annually were just kept in prisons for life, instead of being killed. Abolition – humanitarian considerations aside – is far more cost-effective than lottery-type executions. At present the cost of appeals runs to six or seven million dollars per execution. Yet to keep a person behind bars costs twenty to thirty thousand dollars per year; costly, but far less than even the interest on the price of appeals. Abolishing the death penalty would save the taxpayers hundreds of millions of dollars annually. Execution-upon-sentencing would be even cheaper, if we are prepared to ignore civil rights, due process, and judicial errors.

The most horrible option is to continue with the present

system. It is torture to those under sentence, it is financially punishing to the taxpayers, it is a crushing burden to the judicial system, it is no deterrent to potential criminals, and it offers no added protection to the public at large. How will you vote? Increase executions twenty-fold or above, to satisfy an urge to punish wrong-doers? Or save money and reduce the social tensions by abolishing capital punishment in favor of mandatory life imprisonment without parole?

Kent L. Aldershot

Endeavor

Voices

There was a time when I did not hear.
To shut out the sound was not a deliberate act
– I was simply not attuned.
But now it would seem

That I have received an added, inner sense;
A gift of spiritual hearing.
And I can no longer ignore that which resounds in my ears.

It is a sound so subtle, stealthy,
– Yet screechingly penetrating.
It is the sound of voices ...
Voices disembodied;
Voices once distant, insidiously stealing closer ...
Voices of the lonely, the wounded, the hurting;
The casualties of life.
Voices filled with fear.

Voices transported, as it were, on the wings of the wind;
Voices strong enough to demolish every barricade,
And transform to debris each carefully engineered defense.
Like a battering ram they invade my conscience,
And send my newly-awakened spirit into turmoil:
I fly to the four corners of the earth,
But as a bird of prey they pursue my very shadow.

There is no hiding place from such a multitude
Of voices from Death Row.
In unison they could create an entire city!
–'Twould be a city called Condemned ...
To these I MUST respond!

Vi Brighton, LifeLines Co-ordinator for the state of Florida

To Daniel

Something has turned my life upside down –
No – I'm not a little blue girl upside down –
With kittens in my head –

Something has turned my life upside down –
Something that wanders with me through space and
    time –
Something that smells the grass under my fingers –
Something that hears the voices of children laughing –

Something that sees the beauty of sculptured spires –
Something that feels the warmth of a sun from a
    distant land –
Something that touches the beauty of friendship with
    souls just found –

Someone who changes my life – who changes ME –

Someone who knows the silence of the valley –
Someone who sees the frost touch the trees with spiked
    fingers –
Someone who watches the children of innocence dance
    and play –
Someone who finds the beauty of the stars that set one
    free –
Someone who hears the wind and sea and rain –
Someone who remembers the river and the dreams of
    childhood –
Someone who listens to the whispers of those from the
    past who love him –

Someone who uses my ears – who hears my thoughts –
who feels my love –

Daniel

Elizabeth McOwat, LifeLines

A melody of hope

Huddled into the darkest corner
that life had to offer,
I sat silent.

Bruised and beaten from within
I prayed my enemy would not
discover the hiding place within
my mind.

A stranger from a land a life time
away – reached into my darkness
and turned on the light.

Raising my head,
I looked around and there she stood –
a single step away.

Her eyes aglow with love's understanding.

As she offered her hand to help me stand,
she whispered a melody of hope –
comforting, and assuring,
her words gave me life –
and, within the tears that she
has cried for me, I have found
the truest gift of all, a dream that
all my tomorrows will be better than
any yesterday that I have lived ...

Daniel W. Cook, Death Row, Arizona State Prison, Florence

Partings

Funny how she liked to spend time in the shower thinking.
The isolation, quiet rush of water, steamy, unworldly
atmosphere and enclosedness encouraged this. Hot tears
mingled the spray on her face as she laughed at herself –
enjoying an outpouring of grief in total privacy must be one
of life's pleasures, a sort of emotional masturbation. She
pulled herself together. Panic could be kept at bay by
practical thoughts and everyday rituals. She dressed
mechanically and went through to dry her hair as Lisa
bounced in, hair muzzy, the oyster satin nightshirt over her
swelling belly, an anxious smile scanning her face, eyes dark
and concerned. Today they would both enjoy the little act of
love as Mum prepared breakfast exactly as Lisa would wish.
'Taxi's coming at about ten to,' said Lisa, bouncing off to
the bathroom as Anne picked up the empty plates. Keep busy,

that's the thing. Lisa gave her some toiletries to pack, and Anne brought the magazine for the journey. Inside was a message – 'sweet dreams' – and a kiss; pure sentiment but it made Anne feel better.

'There's nothing in there about not smoking during pregnancy,' she said with a laugh. 'No lectures.'

They hugged again – any minute now the taxi would arrive. Suddenly it was a scramble as they both carried things out and gave each other a last hug. Anne waved, and then stupidly waved at the taxi-driver in an absent-minded attempt to appear normal.

The taxi curved around the square and disappeared out of sight, Lisa waving and looking anxiously to see if her mother's face had yet crumpled. Anne suddenly choked and stepped blindly back into the house, the empty house. With smells and signs in every room and every corner, how could she bear it? Lisa and James had bought a house three hundred miles away. Of course there would be visits, holidays and family celebrations, but this was it – her last baby had left the home, the last of five to fly the nest, gone to live their own lives and find happiness with other people.

Anne worked methodically, stripping the bed and putting in the first load of washing. She rearranged the soft toys on the bed before going round with the hoover. She opened the window and gave the pot-pourri a shake and a sniff. The room was nice and sweet, ready to welcome. Anne continued with the absent-minded skill of long practice, her heart wrenched as she gathered the dead, long-stemmed roses into a bunch and stuffed them head first into her rubbish bin. After an hour the first load of washing was on the rack, filling the kitchen with the fresh smell of detergent. She made a cup of tea and sat down to look at her letters, the television set on for company, as usual, with the sound off.

A catalogue offering Dutch bulbs she put aside to look through later. Wayne's letter had the distinctive stamp on the back to say that it was an uncensored letter from Oklahoma State Penitentiary. It felt thin. She opened it carefully, sniffing the inside as she did so, trying to catch the smell that Wayne had told her about, the penitentiary smell, but she didn't think she noticed anything in particular.

Anne read it through once quickly, anxiously, to reassure herself that there was nothing wrong, then settled back to read it properly, balancing her mug of tea on the chairarm. The familiar writing was small and cramped, but easy enough to read, and she marvelled again at how interesting the letters were, considering they were written by one who was locked down for twenty-three hours a day in a small, windowless cell with no outside stimulation except letters and television. He had been totally honest with her about the circumstances of his crimes, and although his education had been limited, he was literate, intelligent and sensitive.

She imagined him sitting in his cell writing across his knees or leaning on the concrete bunk opposite. As she read, it was hard to comprehend that they both lived in the same world, and that world was supposedly sane and civilized.

'The officials here read Parks his thirty-day execution notice today. They tell you what to expect, they want to know who will pick up your body, what witnesses you want to attend – they let you have five of your own witnesses – and how your visits will go for thirty days. They don't allow facial hair and when he went before this committee he had a little hair on his chin and they wouldn't read the thirty-day deal to him until he cut it off. They'll isolate him before long, probably place him in a security cell.

Another Death Row inmate, Randle Robinson, just got an execution date for March 13th. I heard his mother died a day or so after the date was set on him. It's got to be hard for any mother who has a son or daughter on Death Row and no telling how they'll feel if they're executed. Everybody has to live their own lives I guess, but what you do affects your family in a lot of ways and I regret the pain and sorrow I've caused my Mom and family.'

Anne took her cup into the kitchen. It looked windy outside, but rather cloudy. She might risk hanging out the washing – that way she could put in another load and get it finished. She piled the next lot into the washer and had a mental image of exactly where the train was on its journey south. Anne always felt uneasy until Lisa's reassuring telephone call. She put out the washing, stepping carefully over the grass in her houseslippers as the wind tugged encouragingly.

Shivering slightly, she turned up the gas fire and sat down to re-read Wayne's letter. He was beginning to open up a little, in a way he had been reluctant to do in the beginning. After eighteen years on Death Row he had taught himself to suppress his emotions. He referred to his own appeals which were being prepared by his attorneys:

'I think I may have a chance to get a modification of my death sentence somewhere down the line, but the way the courts are now, especially the US Supreme Court, your chances aren't very good. Parks had his death sentence overturned by the next highest court to the US Supreme Court, but the state appealed and the US Supreme Court reinstated it and you can see where he is now. I don't worry about it, just do what I can on my case, and if I'm executed, I'm executed – nobody lives forever. I've got no chance of ever getting free legally and if I had to live the rest of my life in prison – execution holds no fear for me. Of course, I've never been one to give up or lay down and just let something happen, but I look at things the way they really are.'

He'd signed off the letter in his usual way, 'Take care, Wayne'.

She stared, lost in thought, picturing him in his grey, windowless cell, struggling with his appeal preparation, writing letters, getting news on the grapevine about the latest developments on Death Row. He would hear the guards rehearse the coming execution of Parks, and see Parks move into the isolation cell next door to the execution chamber, with its table and armrests to secure the arms ready for the lethal injection. She thought of Parks and Robinson, of time ticking away relentlessly, and of Robinson's mother and her final, unbearable agony.

'Should I write to George Bush again?' She then decided on another option. She would write to Barbara Bush, a woman like herself, a mother who would surely have understanding and compassion. As she tearfully opened the writing pad, Anne thought about her own pregnant daughter with a small stab of panic, then about Robinson's mother. Some partings were more painful than others.

Joan Warren, LifeLines

To kill or how to kill
In the wake of the film *Execution Protocol*
(To A. J. Joe Doyle)

Fort Potosi – antiseptic five-star chill.
San Quentin – fair castle upon the hill.
   Is there no limit to deception's gimmick
Shrouding dead secrets of justified ills?

Vain hopes abated, the stern eye evades
Corridors mocking where all hell pervades ...
   The inner sanctums – harboring phantoms
Of ghosts long banished to eternal parades.

On Capitol Hill – white city of sages
Where honor and deceit have contrived for ages,
   Appeals in abundance – denied in an instant
Thrust case upon case into archival pages.

Nine judicial peers empowered in black
Head-counting at random which Appeal to attack.
   Innocent or guilty? – Time versus Penalty?
Epitaphs in blood to their much learnèd knack.

Blind retribution belies tech-sophistry
Execution protocol excels execution history.
   The waiting immeasurate – their devising elaborate
Murderous inventions surpassing all witchery.

Lynchings and burnings, once the crudest compulsions,
Now – cyanide pellets stage barbarous convulsions ...
   Slow creeping gasses – engulfing in masses
To strangle, to agonize to depths of repulsion.

Lethal and measured, drip cylinders three
Clocked to the minute, inject travesty
   Their guilt to expiate – as mourners nauseate.
Justice administered in the basest degree

While high voltage charges propelled in the chair
Consume internally all those who would dare.
The dead moan – undying, their spirit – defying
The Leuchters, the butchers ... in final despair.

Survival in the wild, by far, pales in gravity.
Beasts play by rules. The System – depravity!
Preyed on by predator – REVENGE HAILS THE VICTOR!
Trophies the hangman acquires with alacrity.

Esther Gilder, LifeLines

An eyewitness to a murder

Don Eugene Harding was executed in Arizona's gas chamber
on April 6, 1992, beginning at 12.18 a.m., just over a week
ago. I knew Don for about eight months prior to his execution.
Don had asked me to witness his execution so that I might
tell his family and the families of others on Death Row what
actually happens when one is killed by lethal gas. Despite
strong apprehensions, I agreed to honor his request.

Upon my arrival at Arizona State Prison, Florence, Arizona,
I was escorted by a prison official to the chapel where other
witnesses for Don Harding were waiting. As a group, we
avoided talking about what we were about to see. Instead, we
shared memories of our personal human experiences with
Don and his family, and spoke about carrying out his final
wishes. We were in the chapel for nearly an hour, during
which time a prison official had us draw numbers from a box.
This number established the order in which we would enter
into the viewing area and where we would stand in proximity
to the viewing windows of the gas chamber. I drew number
eighteen.

At approximately midnight, all the witnesses for Don, for
the state and from the media, converged on the sidewalk to
walk over to the death house. No one spoke. The only noises
I could hear were my own footsteps and the sounds from
some inmates in the darkened cellblocks hollering at us as
we passed by their windows. We filed into the death house

in the pre-designated order, as a prison staff member checked off our lottery numbers. I stood in the second of three rows, directly behind where Don was seated in the gas chamber. Three sides of the octagonal gas chamber had windows for viewing. As we entered and took our places, the blinds were drawn. When all the witnesses were assembled, an official announced that Don's last appeal had failed and the execution would proceed. The door to the death house viewing room was closed and an officer was ordered to roll up the blinds.

Don was strapped to the metal chair with numerous black restraints. He was facing away from us, dressed only in his underwear. I had been warned in advance of the ritualistic execution policies, and observed my fellow witnesses take on behavior which could only be described as 'execution etiquette': an unspoken but pervasive feeling that we were expected to act civilly and with detachment to the coming events. However, I was struck with a feeling of overwhelming despair as Don Harding, in the name of our government, had indeed been literally and figuratively stripped of his humanity.

I watched Don turn to look at one of his attorneys. He forced a slight smile, but could not disguise the child-like terror in his face. He turned the other direction and I believe he was looking for me. He never knew I was there, as he could not see the people standing directly behind him. He moved around in his chair, as much as the restraints would allow. He seemed to be mumbling to himself. He was agitated and fidgety. Knowing Don as I did, I realized that his agitation was born of his tragic desire to control one tiny aspect of this utterly dehumanizing spectacle. He wanted it to be quick and painless.

About 60 seconds after the blinds were lifted, the pellets were released under his chair. I heard the loud noise as they were dropped into the acid. It took about 5 seconds for the mist, and the first trace of fumes to reach him. At that point, Don's naked back inflated against the chair as if he took a deep breath. His head was thrown back violently against the chair and he turned his head from side to side. He jerked and twisted as if gasping for air. At the same time, his body buckled against the straps. Severe convulsing began, and continued throughout. Even through the thick glass of the gas chamber, I heard him moan a low, guttural sound of sheer torment. I prayed for him to go quickly.

At one point, I was unable to sustain watching this prolonged suffering alone. I broke from my assigned standing spot and walked over to Don's minister. We held on to each other and with his arm around my shoulder, I noticed how badly I was shaking. From that position I could closely see Don's hand and arm were twitching. For the almost two minutes I stood there, his hand never stopped contorting in bizarre ways. His body, especially his back and neck, had turned a deepening red. His head flung back and then dropped against his chest. The convulsions caused his body to shake so badly that I momentarily thought the chair would shake. The spasms and gasping lasted about 7 minutes until his head dropped to his chest for the last time. Finally, he appeared to be dead, but I noticed what appeared to be involuntary movement of his left hand. I continued to pray that this spectacle be over.

I saw a prison doctor approach the glass from the other side of the chamber, in front of Don. He gazed dispassionately at Don's now-quieted body and quickly moved away from the window and back into the shadows on the front side of the chamber. Soon, a prison official announced to the witnesses that the execution was complete. It had taken ten and one-half minutes. The last look at Don was one I will never forget. Where minutes before his body had been hot red, it was now slumped over and was ashen grey/beige – the antiseptic color of the gas chamber itself. The prison officials ordered the blinds to be closed. The door to the outside opened and we filed out.

Nothing in my life prepared me to witness the prolonged, ritualistic torture of another human being. I have struggled to put this experience into any kind of human perspective. I had spent a lot of time imagining painful death before. My father burned to death in a plane crash when I was 21 years old. He died brutally and his body was charred beyond recognition. I am still plagued – twenty-three years later – by gruesome images of his unspeakable suffering in the last painful seconds of his life. Nonetheless, as I watched the agony suffered by Don Harding, I knew that his torment was far worse and much more prolonged than that experienced by my father. I am told that my father probably died in 30 seconds. Don endured his torture for ten and one-half minutes. His suffering was palpable and sickening, and I felt it like a cloak draped over my body. I winced with every convulsion, moan, and every desperate contortion. Those ten and one-half minutes were the longest and most harrowing moments of my life.

A little more than a week later, I am still in shock over what I witnessed. I awake during the night startled and unable to sleep because of the terrifying images of Don suffocating to death. The images of his convulsing and with his hand clenched to the chair will be etched in my mind forever.

I am humiliated for my fellow man. Don's punishment was to torture him in view of 25 witnesses. It was not the act of civilized people. He suffered in discernible agony for over ten minutes. I talked with Don's family about his execution, but I could not bring myself to tell them just how brutally he died. Death by gas is barbaric, and an inhumane infliction of torture.

Donna Leone Hamm

For you

I will climb a tree for you
and in a cave of verdant green
from which sweet, secret, forked retreat
smell sweet air of the free for you
as my heart beats for you.

I will walk in the rain for you
wet warm will soothe, as nature's balm
re-fragrances the earth with dew,
soothing, seeping through each space –
and I will thirst for you.

I will feed the birds for you
and watch, as roses blush and bloom,
each blade of grass shoot green towards the blue.
While I can taste the green upon the tongue –
I'll taste for you – and photosynthesise while I am young.

While I can watch the seasons come and go
and snow can show the robins to and fro,
As winter puts a hush upon the earth –
for what it's worth – I'll watch for you
and see the evening star shine through the midnight blue.

And I can feel the wind for you
and keenly cold, I will grow old
raw nosed, red eared, I'll brave the east,
the piercing east which strikes right through, for you.
And tears which run on ruddy cheeks,
I'll weep for you, I'll weep for you.

I will bed and board for you
and spend for you and hoard for you,
and taste and touch and see and such,
and much, much more for you.
I'll bite and chew
and hack and hew
at life,
for life ... for you.

Joan Warren, LifeLines

VISITING TIME:

LOVE AND FRIENDSHIP

It is sweet to dance to violins
  When Love and Life are fair:
To dance to flutes, to dance to lutes
  Is delicate and rare:
But it is not sweet with nimble feet
  To dance upon the air!

Oscar Wilde

Love through the ultimate barrier: a visit on Death Row

I walk in and step into the closet-sized steel-mesh cage. You're already sitting, waiting on the other side. I stand facing you while the escort uncuffs me.

Arriving in shackles no longer embarrasses me. Sometimes I think they would have us on leashes too, if they could get away with it. I never thought wearing handcuffs would become a way of life.

You're looking so pretty and loving, as usual. I look into your eyes and become entranced by your affection and beauty, forgetting all that I'd planned to say – yet what's left to say?

Can't we touch? 'Just one little touch, Warden?' Yeah ... I'm dreaming again.

There are only two hours we're allowed to share together, although we're separated by reinforced glass and steel wire-mesh and aren't really 'together'. Still, when I look into your tender expression I see no reason for words. Your eyes say it all.

I see in your face the secrets we've shared, the love we've felt. In your eyes, a reflection of me.

As I try with all my being to completely absorb your essence – through sight and sound alone – the image multiplies, trickling down your cheek in each tear of loving, frustrated passion.

The liquid treasure is wiped away by delicate hands, to be stored somewhere deep within until some hoped-for, far-away day. All the torment. All the desire. All the tiny reflections of me. If only I could be the tissue for your tears ...

We talk a little but the conversation seems strained and unimportant. I want to keep you entertained for the short two hours but my imagination stretches only so far. How much could I have to talk about, living my life in a 5' by 9' barred room? Once again we end up sharing our dreams, fantasies and desires.

'You've got five more minutes!' the guard announces.

The bright, reflective eyes immediately cloud over. Reality

seems to cut a little deeper and sting a little harder each time. Liquid love is flowing once more.

The first five – wondering what to say and do. The last five – trying to prepare for that excruciating moment of walking out different doors, in opposite directions.

It's only a door, a fence, a reinforced glass window and steel mesh, yet it's infinity stretched between us.

I often wish you could relate to what I feel – understand my emotions – and loss of emotion. The sadness and regrets never depart.

You look past me. The guard comes and unlocks the door on the small cage. We say our 'I love you's' but never a goodbye. Just the word, goodbye, seems to carry a bad omen on Death Row.

I stand to be cuffed, backing out still looking at you. You try to leave with grace, but I doubt there could ever be any.

In the back room, while undressing to be strip-searched, I am silent. Happy but sad. Cuffed once more, I am escorted back to my 5′ by 9′ where so many thoughts race through my mind. Now I remember all the things I wanted to say and ask.

I sit on my bunk looking at myself in a tiny mirror. It's like I'm looking at you again. It's the same reflection I saw in your eyes and in your tears. It comes to me that each of your shimmering tears are drops of medicine … the only medicine I know that's capable of healing my wounded heart.

Death Row inmate, Huntsville, Texas

12–31–91 at 10:57:49*

i wish there were bars
in this prison
or clanging keys doors
something
to make the others angry
like i am
and aware
that there are no murals

in the sky
no graphite-sketched afros
of sisters on
the walls
no native american history
stretched across the desert of
these thoughts
no primal screams are heard
of the burials
with love
it is only that of me
thinking of you
and pain colored rue.

*Central standard time (meaning it is just about midnight on the East Coast – where it counts!)

Harold L. Otey, Death Row,
Nebraska State Penitentiary, Lincoln

The family visit

The sun rose steadily that spring morning, its brilliant rays gradually replacing the harsh glow of the security lamps that are spread throughout the compound on Tennessee's Death Row; lamps so intense that my cell must be one of the nation's most secure prison facilities, giving the impression of an endless summer night in the Arctic.

It's 5.45 a.m. as I wake to watch the sun break free of the hold held on it by the horizon. The security lamps go off; in return the fluorescent lights come on within the unit. Another day begins, illuminated inside and out, so as to expose every move and thought. Today is a visiting day and I have every reason to be overwhelmed with excitement. But the realization of the all-too-quick ending to the few hours spent with my family takes its toll on my passion. My emotions seesaw between the anticipated joy of being with my loved ones and the knowledge that this will be followed by the pain of total separation that their leaving will bring.

One hour later finds me in the shower anxiously trying to

scrub away the institutional aroma that clings naturally to a building housing ninety-six condemned men. It is forever my heart's desire to be as pure as possible for my visits. After all, my family and I serve my sentence together and this monthly visit needs to be in order if we wish to 'escape' this concrete and steel jungle, even if it is only for a few short hours.

As the squelch of the officer's radio is broken I overhear the announcement of the arrival of my visitors, 'Visitation officer to Unit 2 – inmate Hutchison has a visit'. The rattle of keys and approaching footsteps alert me to prepare for the required strip-search. Entering the visitation gallery with my heart in my throat it is all I can do to take a seat. The echoes bouncing off the bare walls and the glaring streaks of light reflected from the round observation mirrors seem to penetrate and expose my every thought.

The slamming of doors quickens my spirit; a warm smile covers my face, evaporating any traces of my tears. I eagerly await my family as they sign in. We greet one another with hugs and kisses, taking advantage of a special closeness that so many families in the free world take for granted. The visit time is short but sweet. Of the 8,760 hours in each year, the fifty or so that we can devote to visits clearly exemplify the extremely disproportional role that numbers play in our lives. Such one-sided ratios as 14 hours out of 168 that are allowed for outside exercise, 15 minutes in the shower and one weekly phone call spring to mind.

The visit ends and my family and I struggle with our goodbyes. We try to stand strong and faithful, putting all our efforts into suppressing any show of emotion, only to fail miserably as evidenced by the tears that are slung as we turn sharply to depart. The long walk back to my cell is not as lonely as one might imagine, for my thoughts are reverberating preciously with the touch and sounds of a loving family.

After another strip-search the oversized metal door at the entrance to my cell closes with mighty authority, sealing me for another period of time. The noon meal is waiting for me, packaged all nice and neatly in the sort of plastic trays usually containing hamburgers in fast-food restaurants. How ironic that the state of Tennessee provides us with the best of nourishment and care only to sustain us unto death! Yet so many of the homeless go without food in the very city that borders this institution.

As the afternoon rolls around a restless stirring is obvious within the unit. Yard time consists of two hours spent with other inmates inside a wire-meshed concrete-floored pen. The time is passed making phone calls, playing cards, chess or basketball. Myself and others are usually found in groups together, sharing our thoughts and insights. The fresh air and the scenery of surrounding rolling ridges serve to take me back to simpler times, once again providing an 'escape' from this otherwise harsh environment. As usual this 'escape process' is centered around and rooted in my family – the smell of the freshly mown grass within the compound, the sound of distant automobile traffic and the caress of a warm breeze all seem to transport me back home.

But reality bites hard and before I know it yard time comes to an end. Like a herd of cattle we are all driven back to our cells; the day has peaked, the meager excitement has wavered and I sense that demon called loneliness stalking from the darkness, waiting, watching and willing to leap upon its prey. It is at these times that I am thankful for the promises of a living and faithful God.

Returning from the yard I rush to prepare for tonight's worship service. The service is held in the visitation area and the memories of this day's visit with my family seize my heart and soul when I enter the room. Just the thought of having sat here earlier, sharing time with my loved ones, is almost too much to bear.

Toward the end of the service we all shake hands and say our goodbyes. Then we march back into our cells with the knowledge that we made it another day. Later on that night I wince as the harsh security lamps fire up once again. But tonight is different as I drift more easily to sleep – for, you see, today I had a family visit.

Olen E. Hutchison, Death Row,
Nashville, Tennessee

Make a difference

what do you know about
slumlords capitalism
(why there are) child molesters, wife beaters
gestapo police judges attorney generals
those who legally kill
what do you know about
the self-professed the know-it-all the fearing the un-neutral
who say lesbians are bad mothers
those gays not human to wear manly the uniform
the only criminals end up in prisons
what do you know about
people who steal
people who mug
people who rape
people who only want respect
what do you know about
living in a ghetto slum housing where
roaches rats maggots hip hop hooray
hearing yourself complain
having to prepare the rotten meat
the butcher sold that usda approved
your family used foodstamps used
no longer arguable
what do you know about
the drive-by shootings funerals
the crack dealers running the neighborhood burials
the schools that look like alcatraz funerals
churches liquor stores bars cadillac burials
what do you know about
making revolution
making a baby (who might survive this century;
hell, this day) making anyone know you are alive
really
what do you know about
swelling up to be
crying to be

pleading to be
pretending to believe
you can
forget the self
just love
to make a difference.

Harold L. Otey, Death Row,
Nebraska State Penitentiary, Lincoln

The final visit

The road to Angola, Louisiana's State Penitentiary, twists and turns towards the largest prison in the USA. The road ends at the prison, an 18,000 acre plantation, bounded on three sides by the Mississippi River and on the fourth by the rattlesnake infested Tunica Hills. The heat is unbearable, over 100 degrees with humidity to match. Outside the gates is a little 'caff', a scene from 'The Good, the Bad and the Ugly', a place that Vi Brighton got to know very well for the three days I was visiting inside Death Row.

Way back in February I promised to visit my friend, Andrew Lee Jones, when his previous stay was granted. So, here I was to keep that promise. Andrew had so looked forward to 'setting down for a good conversation' and was so excited at my arrival in Angola. It was to be a sad, anxious and strangely happy few days for everyone who cared about Andrew, his family, his friends, lawyers and himself. I visited him on two days while the lawyers spent time with his family trying to get a stay on various issues. Vi and I visited his mother, Hazel, and met his brothers and sisters, filling gaps in my knowledge of Andrew's life. The day of the Pardon Board hearing was long and hot and I was allowed to plea for Andrew's life. The Board voted 3:2 to defer execution to lethal injection, but the Governor overrode them and determined that Andrew should die by electrocution despite the well known problems with the electric chair.

On Sunday, I joined Andrew and his family for the last four hours of visiting and we all kept up his spirits, particularly his brave and strong sisters. At 6 p.m. we all left cheerily at Andrew's request, and collapsed in grief outside the building. Vi and I spent the night with the family. At 12.10 a.m. on July 22nd, Andrew was declared dead. He was the last person in the state to be executed by electrocution.

Andrew had spent 7 years on Death Row following a trial at which he was inadequately represented and where only circumstantial evidence was offered. He was given 9 execution dates during his time on Death Row.

Despite this, Andrew never felt bitter towards anyone for his fate and believed that had his life circumstances been different, he would not be on Death Row. He went to his death without bitterness. During his lifetime he gave love to many people and especially his family, and he is still remembered by his friends as a regular guy who enjoyed practical jokes, would always give whatever he had to help a friend and was just fun to be with.

The man I met was the friend I had been writing to, only more so. He was thoughtful, kind and gentle. He held no grudges against anyone despite the many irregularities about his original trial. He was NOT the man that the state had condemned to die in 1984. Everyone, except the Governor and the prosecution, agreed that he deserved the chance of a retrial. The experience for me was, I hope, unique, and it has certainly confirmed my horror of capital punishment and its harsh effects on everybody involved. Who will give comfort to Hazel, Andrew's mother, and his family? Will the family of the victim really feel satisfaction? I doubt it. As for me, I have lost a dear and valued friend. I miss telling him the news from England and the things I do, the colours, sights and smells of a free life.

Thank you, Andrew. Be in peace my friend.

ANDREW LEE JONES 24.8.55–22.7.91

Jane Officer, founder of the Andrew Lee Jones Fund

Endeavor

Reflections

I sit here in this lonely cell,
I think of all the lost dreams that I once had,
I think of what it would be like to be free once again.
I often wonder where did I take the wrong turn in life.
For my life has been with more downs than ups,
No man, woman or child should live the way I have lived,
For at times I never had a purpose,
I lived only to encounter risks.
For I always felt to take a risk I could learn how to be
    brave.
But look at me now,
For my risks and bravery have me sitting here on DEATH
    ROW.

❖   ❖   ❖

A man without hope is a man without a dream.
And without a dream a man has no purpose.
To be here on Death Row a man needs something to keep
    him alive.
For I feel at times that I don't have a purpose.

But I do have dreams and hopes.
For one day I'll be able to put the life on the Row behind
    me.
To be able to go on without the thought of not having a
    purpose.
For I have been lonely, sad, I even tried to be happy here.

But tell me, how can a man be happy with the thought of
    his life
Being ended with the push of a button?
How can I help but keep the thought of not having a
    purpose?
For my life here I live without the thought of a tomorrow,
Now and today is what I must justify with.

For if I try to think of a tomorrow it only comes down to
    one thing,
Sad, lonely and without a purpose.

Andrew Lee Jones

Andrew Lee Jones was executed in Louisiana in 1991.

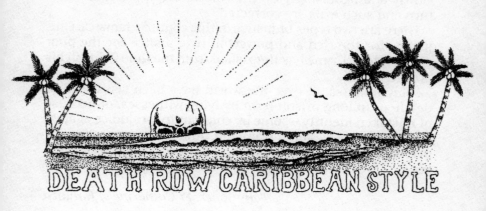

DEATH ROW CARIBBEAN STYLE

And as one sees most fearful things
  In the crystal of a dream,
We saw the greasy hempen rope
  Hooked to the blackened beam,
And heard the prayer the hangman's snare
  Strangled into a scream.

And all the woe that moved him so
  That he gave that bitter cry,
And the wild regrets, and the bloody sweats,
  None knew so well as I:
For he who lives more lives than one
  More deaths than one must die.

Oscar Wilde

The death penalty

No-one know how often innocent persons have been convicted for a crime of murder, but it always happen. Only slowly and agonisingly do the wheels of justice sometimes turn and such evils are corrected.

There are two types of justice in this country, Jamaica. One, justice for the rich and powerful, two, justice for the poor and helpless. Crime has flourished from the time Cain kill his brother 'Abel'.

Many inmates all over the world have been sentenced to death, *or* to long prison term by lying witnesses, *or* because of mistaken identity – some by community prejudice against the person, *or* by some frame-up. And many times, too, by over-zealousness of the police to find a suspect to solve a case.

Tony Jones, St Catherine's, Jamaica

Dark time

It is a dark time my love
The sun is sinking beyond the sky
Flowers, trees, bow their heads
The music of birds is slow
A spectacle name Death Row

Dry up you tears now youth man
Loose your belly band mother
Away beyond the dark and murky fog
There is a radiant beam of light
Shining for you and for men

Charles Lowther, St Catherine's, Jamaica

Conditions on Death Row in Trinidad

The condition/treatment has gotten worse. Approximately 23 hours, 30 minutes I am kept in this cell each day, which is badly ventilated. The cell is 8′ × 8′, cold/filthy. This is what takes place here on Death Row every day until my innocence is proven. The prisoners could either read books, magazines or newspaper if he can get them and if he can read. Write letters, that's if you can afford postage and stationery, and if you can read. Look out a small vent in your cell door or walk back and forth the short distance (8′ × 8′) of his cell or sit/lie thinking. Sleep (sometimes trying to sleep).

I am further made to suffer stink from three out of order toilets just a few feet behind the cell. I am also made to keep my bucket (toilet) with faeces and urine for as long as 10–12 hours daily in the cell. I'm also made to brush my teeth and wash my face over the bucket. I have to sometimes go for days without anything to eat because the commissioner is saying he is not getting any money from the government to feed condemned prisoners. I get one hour exercise per week, any one of the days they choose, during the week. Sometimes we don't get. This exercise is done with handcuff on your hand throughout the exercise. Could you imagine exercising with handcuffs on? There is nothing for you to do but to stand and talk with a fellow inmate or watch the sky. When having your bath a prison officer has to watch you, this behaviour is very inhuman. The bucket takes up most of the time you have to bathe because one has to clean it, or bring it back in your cell filthy. As the cell size is 8′ × 8′ much care must be taken in cleaning the bucket in order to maintain proper hygiene. Each prisoner is allowed out of the cell merely to collect his meals tray and back to his cell (that's if they have food to give). The cells are separated by walls; each cell has a wood door with a hole in it, 9" × 3", and that hole is still blocked with wire, so you will be looking through the wire to see the corridor. You could communicate with the prisoner directly opposite you and sometimes the cell opposite don't have to have a prisoner in it. The bed, wood bench, table and bucket takes up all the space in the cell. We are subjected to three searches of both cells and body each day. The final search is 9.30 p.m. so you can't go to sleep before that time. In addition to this torment the lights are kept on during the entire day and night. My prolonged incarceration and the cruel and unusual treatment is violating the rights I have under the prison regulation and the constitution of my country.

For almost two months now the prison authorities haven't gave us no toothpaste to brush our teeth. I have to beg other prisoner who get visits regularly for some. They gave us one soap to bathe for two weeks, each prisoner gets one. This place is getting from bad to worse here.

When the diet tray comes, it comes with roaches all over it. You could see them clearly. They give us a yellow peas full of worms sometimes. The bread we get are stale. I get accustomed to eating this stale bread because I don't get visit often and I have to eat something to survive. Some of the guys here family comes every week and buy things for them to eat. I am not that lucky so I have to eat something. I eat the stale bread, butter or jam. Sometimes they give us tea (with no milk). I drink some tea in the afternoons. If they give me any different peas from the yellow peas I will sometime eat some.

The prison is badly in need of medication. All kinds of things comes out on your skin. And you have to beg to see the prison doctor who comes into the prison when he feels like. When my sister visit me, she brings some fruits for me, and if she has money she will buy some things at the canteen for me. I have to save whatever she buys because sometime when the food comes no prisoners eats it, it just can't be eaten.

There are some very wicked officers here, who will beat you for anything. I have never gotten beaten up by them. When they beat you some part of your body *must* break. If they find this letter, I will be beaten badly. So you could understand what a chance I am taking. Writing this letter I am even frightened. I am fed up seeing guys get beat up here, for nothing.

I listen to other guys talk and all they talk about is revenge and killings. I don't like to hear them talk about these things, but this is the way the prison officers (some) and prison conditions makes you feel.

Leroy James, Death Row, Trinidad

He does not sit with silent men
  Who watch him night and day;
Who watch him when he tries to weep,
  And when he tries to pray;
Who watch him lest himself should rob
  The prison of its prey.

Oscar Wilde

Death watch

Some of you, I'm sure, are aware of the procedure of carrying out the executions here in Texas. Men are taken from the Ellis 1 Unit to the Walls Unit in Huntsville, where the executions are done.

What you may not be aware of is here on Ellis 1, when you are within forty-eight hours of your execution date, you are removed from the cell you have been living in and placed in the Death Watch Cell. There are two of these cells in G-13 Wing.

I have been on other wings when they removed men, taking them to Death Watch. When on the other wings, where there is no contact with men in Death Watch, it becomes something in the back of your mind.

Living now in G-13, the men being moved to Death Watch suddenly have a very dramatic impact on everyone living here.

You see, the Death Watch cells are the first two cells on the flag (the bottom tier). They happen to be right in front of our recreation day room. This means if you are in the day room, each time you look up through the windows, you are looking right into the bare cells called Death Watch. More often than I care to think, when you glance across you will be looking into the face of someone in these cells.

This is so hard, you want to walk over where one small window has been removed (so hot water can be passed into the day room for the men in the day room to make a cup of coffee) and talk with the person on Death Watch, but what can you say, good luck??

When they put someone on Death Watch they take all their property with the exception of their legal work and Bible. So a person is just there in a bare cell.

Moving men to Death Watch doesn't really make any sense. It's supposed to be so they can watch you, to make sure you don't hurt yourself, but that is ridiculous, guards don't pay any attention to men in these cells. This makes me feel like moving someone to Death Watch is just another way to make the whole process more painful.

This cell is also where you are given your last meal. I've seen guards bring the last meals to several of these men. Regardless of what is ordered, very little is ever eaten.

Not long after the last meal is served, the person is removed from the cell and taken to Huntsville for the last few hours. This is very hard to watch, these men in the Death Watch cells. It is even harder if the person in the Death Watch cell happens to be someone you know and have come to like.

I have written this article to give you readers an insight into another part of this madness.

Also I have written this to, in a small way, let the men know that find themselves in Death Watch, when you look across into the day room and guys don't quite meet your eyes and never have a lot to say, it's not that they don't care my friends, it's just that they feel your pain also.

Claude 'BJ' Jones, Death Row, Huntsville, Texas

Death-watching*

i sat in one-room world
in t-shirt marked hospital
brown khaki pants used white socks and shower shoes
greeted faces which
substantiated souls
some talked
a lot silently wept
most hugged out good-byes
and i thought
this is your last day
on this earth alive
what do you believe in
why do you not tremble
sob shiver shake grow angry
what will you remember about
this life
this day these people this person
death-shooing i would squeeze a hand
look into eyes

ogle the casio watch
think of you there
the loyalty commitment sacrifice
to boldface love this last moment with
the pain when night would come
as 10 o'clock emptied my
world i stood up to witness
the difference between the real and unreal
through the cell window screened black-painted steel
gloom saw out over the parking lot
the sunset earlier filmed by camera crews
predicting events to be ...
the skies unleashed
no rip van winkle thunder
of ten-pins rolling
no bone-chilling claps
as if applause were universally acknowledging
just straight rain slashing through
darkness turning white sleeted
directed lightning
justifiable hurled from above
i reflected
this was the night for death to die
the nebraska sable blanket like moonglow
what my great-aunt once said
occurred only when righteous folk
were burying the dead and heaven would
burst open the skies and send the angels down
to escort that soul up into the kingdom
in front of the throne and tears would rain
down upon the earth to let the mourners those departed
know that peace serenity was again to be
the word was life anewed and truth
recorded without thunder without fanfare
a bigger plan to lead with the light

Harold L. Otey, Death Row,
Nebraska State Penitentiary, Lincoln

The poet was to be executed this night.

Surviving an execution date

It sounds senseless that a civilized state, in the name of Justice, can nowadays be so barbaric at some of its citizens, driving them along a slow, well organized route of sadistic torture to finally extermine them as a solution to cure criminality. No words will ever express what it is like to go through an execution date, what follows endeavors to bring a testimony.

Tuesday, February 9, 1993. 8.15 a.m. I can not remember what was the weather like on this day. I was cold, I had not slept much. My body and my mind were under an intense pressure. I was trying hard to get rid of it; this day looked to be a long one and I could not fail in what I expected from myself: give Sam the support and the comfort he needed on the very strenuous way of his 6th execution date.

The last visit
Fifteen years on Death Row, a serious date, indeed, one minute after midnight, tonight ... I am sitting alone in the waiting room of Ellis 1 Unit, next to the visiting room. I know what I have to do: push the fear, the anguish to the side so my usual inner peace will be the only owner of the place. Easier to say than to do ... But reminding the courage, the dignity and the wisdom that Sam showed when we met the days before blows my stress out. He needs me strong and smiling, not weak and sad. I get up and I walk straight to the place I was assigned, attracting the compassionate attention of the few other visitors who know what I have to deal with. Sam appears, his hands cuffed behind his back, he enters the cage, the guard locks it, removes the cuffs through a small window. Sam can then sit down and we are face to face, a thick wired glass partition between us. We smile and look deeply at each other to make sure that our hope is well alive and that we have the situation under control. We both admit that we did not sleep much. The day before, at about 12.30 a.m., he was moved to the death watch cell after all his property had been taken from him: *'The guards came every 15 minutes to write down all I did, all I drank, ate, used the*

toilet stool, pee or fell asleep ... whatever I did was written down. This also continued all night long. At 2.45 a.m. on the 9th, I was awaken for breakfast ... I ate little and the guards watched what I ate and wrote it down.'

Sam's life is now in the hands of the US Supreme Court for the second time in a little more than four years. On December 12, 1988, he already made the trip to the Death House, to be executed at the first minute of the next day and a stay was granted 1h20 before the limit. Sam and I do not lie to each other; we share fully how we feel: tired, stressed, painful but still hopeful and ready to go through those dark hours knowing that the decision of the Supreme Court will come late for the best or for the worst. We both have the will to stay strong whatever it takes, well aware that it will be a constant struggle and that the time going by, the pressure will intensify. Some of his family flew from Georgia and Florida. They have not seen Sam for years. They join us some twenty minutes later. I listen to the moving words Sam has to his children, back to him very recently, telling them that if he was to die in the coming hours, he expects them to be good, honest, to always have the right behavior, to love people and to have no place for hatred in their heart. All day long, he has words of wisdom and of love at all of us. But as the time is going by, I can see how hard he is struggling; so much suffering appears on his face from time to time. The glass partition is more oppressing than it has ever been and I feel so powerless in comforting him. No man to reach out to a helping hand; no shoulder to lean on, no hug, a total deprivation of physical contacts for years. This is never permitted, not even at the last minute.

The trip to the death house
At 3.00 p.m., much earlier than expected, the guards come to take Sam for the dreadful trip to the Walls, the old prison where the executions are carried out, downtown Huntsville. *'On the way to the Death House, my hands and feet are shackled; the warden and another drive behind the van with high powered shotguns. The guards in the van have high powered shotguns.'* Before leaving Ellis 1, somebody tells us that we can go the the Walls Unit and visit Sam until 5.00 p.m.

but when reaching the place, our request is denied and the countdown of the most terrible hours I ever had in my life starts.

The countdown

Sam is now in the hands of the executioners that want so badly to kill him. He is their prey and I am well aware that they will spare him no detail of the deadly protocol of revenge. On January 7, at about 1.00 a.m., he was taken from the cell for a 535 miles trip to Lubbock, the place he was sentenced to die fifteen years ago: *'The sheriff told me, this will be your last trip to Lubbock, you will be executed on February 10th. The captain laughed and asked me, how long are you here? I reluctantly said 15 years ... I then asked to the sheriff, who told you I would die? He said both the attorney general's office and the prosecution office. I said no more but I was moved by his expectation that I would die. When we reached Lubbock, I went in the courtroom and was given the execution date. Immediately I was driven back to Ellis 1 where I arrived about 10.00 p.m.'*

Sam is strong, he believes in God, he even lives in God; also, Sam is realistic and he knows that the date is serious. He is ready to die. I am ready to see him dying, though my pain and the terrible loss I shall have to cope with. We do not fear death, we both believe that it is surely sweeter than the daily life on Death Row he is so tired of, a real mad house that requests a daily struggle to try to keep a balance. But the rite of execution is such a torture that the strongest person in the world can not go through it without being scared.

The questions to deal with in the final hours

I drive the family back to the Hospitality House, the place they are housed and where more than accommodation is provided to those visiting the prisoners, a warm comforting atmosphere that is truly priceless in such circumstances. At that time, Sam is going through the steps of the deadly rite: *'They told me to shower, so I did. They gave me a blue shirt and pants. I refused the meal. They finger printed me. I was placed in a yellow 5' × 9' holding cell, wire screen ... Two guards sat in chairs directly in front of the cell facing me non stop. There was no privacy and when I sat on the toilet stool they remain looking even when I wipe my ass. The guard told me where and when I would be buried. From that point I waited and waited and hoped for a stay while the prison minister told me how I would die. The warden came and told me in a demanding way how I would die and what they expected from me in a way of participation.'* Same words as four years ago: *'The warden told me I would be killed and when, and how. He said, participate and die easily or resist and suffer more. He said, we shall strap you to a gurney, eight straps, put needles in both arms in your veins. Solutions shall flow through your veins until you are dead. You shall be permitted to have very brief last words.'*

Do you understand what will happen to you?
Do you have any questions?
What do you want for a last meal?
Do you plan to make a last statement?
What do you want us to do with your body?
What do you want to do with your property?
Who do you want to have your money?
Who will witness your execution?
Do you know what we expect you to do?
Are you comfortable?
If not, what can we do?
If your stay is denied, who do you want to call?
What color clothes do you want to die in?

Those are the questions all Death Row prisoners have to answer in the final hours.

The death chaplain

Sam is alone, two blocks away from us. The family and I talk of him, of the wonderful man they discovered today, of the true love he radiates. We talk of the past events that drove him on Death Row, we read the newspapers describing him as a monster, forgetting to release the explanations, the mitigating evidence of his case that could help people to understand why he came to do wrong. But it is easier to execute when you make people believe that society gets rid of a man who is not a human being. I am lost in my thoughts. Somebody rings at the door. A prison minister comes in. He introduces himself as 'the death chaplain'. He has no compassion, no comforting words, he is on job and he wants to talk to the three of us who will witness the execution. He takes us in the next room and tells us that he does not like this situation, that he is not responsible for the death sentence but he has to give us some details. He says that Sam had his last shower, his last meal, and has been explained how he will be executed and what is expected from him in a way of participation; then he takes out a writing pad and he starts to make a drawing of the death watch cell Sam is locked in, just in front of the death chamber. He draws him strapped on the gurney, escaping not one of the sadistic details such as the numbers of straps he will be tied with, and the place of the hole in the wall through which the tube containing the poison will flow. Then he explains how Sam will be killed: first he will be put to sleep and this is not painful, he said, then his breathing will be blocked, then his heart beatings will be stopped. All this will take a few minutes. 'Some men die easily, some others die hardly,' he said. Then he added some more details to his drawing: the place where we shall stand, behind bars, first row; second row, the authorities; third row, the press. Bars ... No wired glass partition ... For the first time, almost nothing will separate us, but we are told that the distance between the gurney and the bars forbids all physical contacts. 'When you will hear the door slamming, it will be the sign that the execution is starting.'

My heart is beating too fast, I feel dizzy. I just can not believe it. It is about 7.00 p.m., five hours before the time, and the way this man, a minister, is talking to us of Sam's death with such an assertive tone makes our hope faint. Do we really have to know so much, so long in advance? But he is not finished, we have to know about Sam's last will, who will have his property, who will have the few dollars remaining on his inmate account, and most of all, the details of his funerals. 'Sam will be buried tomorrow morning 8.30, at the prison cemetary. He has been asked which color he wants to wear, he has not expressed any.' God, how long will this man speak to us of Sam's death, Sam's funerals, while he is still well alive, struggling hard? But he has not said yet the only thing we really need to know: we are expected at the death house by 11.15 p.m. Then he asks if we have any questions. What could be left? We had more than expected, more than needed ... So he gets up, puts his folder and writing pad back in his attache-case and leaves just like a business man would do after his last meeting of the day.

Keeping my hope alive

It is now time for me to go back to the hotel for interviews. I reluctantly leave the family, we need each other so badly. But I am more than ever determined to speak out. I owe it to Sam and to all the men sharing the same fate. On my way back to the Hospitality House, I am telling myself that I must not let myself be impressed by the staging of Sam's killing. I must struggle as hard as he is, and not give in to fear. It is about 9.00 p.m., now. We are all sitting on the sofa, not far from the phone set. We can hardly speak. Every second brings more pressure, more torture. I have the feeling that my back is against a wall and a monstrous, infernal engine is slowing coming to me. But no way out and it will crush me. No, I shall not kneel, I shall not cry, I shall not faint. I am not alone, we are not alone. So many people we never heard of before, and all the friends from many countries have sent messages of support, and they are now praying with us. Thinking of their love so freely given makes me smile for gratitude. Love is the key. If only the whole world could realize that only true love can heal all its wounds. I am with Sam in mind, the pain is huge, from time to time a dagger sticks deeper in the wound, I am scared but I am still capable of pulling myself together. I muster all my courage, and regain some peace. I can not believe that Sam will die tonight. Why killing a man like him? He has nothing to do with the mentally ill man he was sixteen years ago. Taking his life, imposing on us this terrible suffering, is of no comfort to the family and friends of the victims; it will not make the world safer and it will not prevent another sick man to do what he did. Sam is healed and his only will is to love people, to help them, to share with them the wisdom he gained over the years. Killing him makes no sense.

The phone call

9.55 p.m. The phone rings. The Supreme Court has taken a decision. The pressure at this very moment is incredible. We are paralyzed. Sam is speaking. 'The Supreme Court has granted a stay ... I love you all.' This time we have no reason to keep control on our emotion! We cry, hug, kiss each other. Our happiness is as intense as the pressure was a few seconds earlier. We do not know what will be next. Another execution date? Another trial? But for a few seconds, our joy is not mixed with fear. We would like to rush at the prison, to hug Sam, to talk with him, but this is not permitted and it will take a full week until I can visit him again.

10.30 p.m. I drive back to the hotel to call my family. Though it is 5.30 a.m. in France, I know they are not sleeping. I was so painful those last days thinking that I may have to announce them that Sam was no longer with us. My younger daughter takes the call, she cries joy and I cry with her. I talk to my other daughter, to my mother.

Back to Ellis 1 Unit

Sam is taken back to Death Row, exhausted: *'It was a cruel and tensed, stressful and painful ordeal ... There was much torture, intense and severe stress, much psychological and physical strain. We were stressed and pressured beyond limits. For those who believe in Heaven and Hell, and we do believe there is a better place God has prepared for all who love him, Dominique and I have already been to Hell.'* For the second time in four years, he makes the trip back from the Death House: *'I was placed in an empty cell, no mattress, nothing. But at 1.00 a.m. I received a mattress, sheets, pillow and blankets. No, no, I could not sleep at all. I was drained and exhausted.'*

On Tuesday, February 16, one week after the ordeal, the prison permitted me at last to visit Sam. We shared our happiness but also we both realized that we are no longer the same people we were before this terrible experience. You can never get used to it, no matter how many dates a man can be given. Each on our side, not even permitted to stay together in the last hours, we reached the pit of the sadistic cold terror too many people have to endure. In the final hours, it drove me crazy that there was nobody to call on to have it stopped. Who is really responsible for it? All those who take part in it carefully hide one behind the other. The killing is anonymous. It makes it easier.

Dominique Malon
(with the contribution of Samuel Hawkins; all quotations
printed in italic are excerpts from his letters)

Wall of death

These Walls of Death are filled with
    the souls of the meek and evil
    men of the past.
Their very presence contaminates
    those that dwell within
Their souls cry out with the sounds
    from the sea
Begging feverishly to be set free.

These Walls are not made of glass
    nor wood,
So it is best we understood
What makes them tremble with
    fear when God's hand
Passes over so close and so near.

These Walls bleed as if someone is
    squeezing
The juices of life from the arteries
    of their horrid past,
The darkness is filled with the
    stenchy smell
Of decayed bones and flesh,
Which is only the breath of the
Devil reaching out to us.

These Walls are mankind's unholy
     realities filled
With Earthly personalities,

These are the Walls of inhumane
Democracy.

Lloyd Earl Jackson, Death Row, San Quentin, California

Death watch: the journal of a Florida convict awaiting execution

Friday May 27, 1983
Here it is – a beautiful, sunny, warm, breezy day in Florida –
9.30 a.m. Such a day breathes – smells – epitomizes life; it
blesses the joy of living.

Gov. Bob Graham, by mere stroke of a pen (I so wonder what
it cost) has ordered my execution a second time. As a result
I am awash with tears, frightened, angry, but determined to
struggle.

Last night, unaware of what was to come, I read until my
eyes ached, then prayed before hauling this shattered frame
upon my bunk. Restful sleep arrived in the early morning and
lasted until breakfast came at the regimented hour of 5.30.
Then, because sleep's quiet beauty visits the condemned only
sparingly, I gladly returned to death-like peace.

Groggily I awakened to hear Sgt N and Officer R say, 'They
want you up front.'

'Okay' I muttered. 'Give me a few minutes to get dressed.'

'No. They want you now. And I have to watch you get
dressed.'

At that moment I knew. And oh, how knowledge reminded
self of inferiority. I was – once more – expendable to a society
which holds one's frailties as cause for extermination.

Brushing teeth meticulously and combing hair for what
seemed like hours, I lingered from doom as long as I could.
Trembling, I managed to inform two inmates of the warrant.
Their response, choreographed in unison: 'Things gonna be
all right, Doug.' In the throes of anxiety and disbelief, I was

handcuffed behind and led to the corridor, where two escorts 'greeted' me. On trembling legs I trekked through the general prison population. Moving through the wings, I was struck by the disproportionate number of black faces and by the city-like setting: filled with people, rushing, loud. The prison 'girls' with painted faces and high falsettos offered propositions – all to the guards' delight.

Inside the assistant superintendent's office, with the superintendent and Death Row classification officer D present, I was treated with 'kindness'. The superintendent asked that the handcuffs be moved to the front, asked if I preferred to sit, asked – in pleasant tones – if I knew the reason for my presence there. He asked of all and everything, yet the question of questions was notably absent: the question of whether I wanted life, God's precious and priceless gift to fallible beings – his children.

With tears streaming, and fighting, literally for breath, I heard the superintendent say, 'The Governor signed your death warrant this morning.'

Then he read the warrant, looked at a calendar and said, 'Let's see ...' And after pondering a few seconds he continued the ritual with the words: 'I've set your execution date for June 21 at 7.00 a.m.'

The superintendent left quickly, and the assistant superintendent made final preparations prior to my being taken to death watch.

He wanted to go over the names of family and friends on my visiting list and provide me with rules and regulations regarding telephone calls. Alarmingly, he asked what clergyman I desired. Poverty-stricken family would visit, of course. And Tony – the gentlest and brightest sort – would be my only visitor as friend. Thinking of such wonderful people, I became aware of renewed strength and vibrancy; determination rose, and with it the will for life.

Someone had to be notified of the death warrant, I was told. With family and Tony at work, I gave Marcia's [Marcia Schwen, a friend] name to the assistant superintendent. The request met with much resistance, of course; but the 'kindness' factor had not perished. Staring at me, looking at my pitiable state, he said I could call 'one time only'. Within the space of thirty minutes, his secretary phoned three times. No response. I then called Bob [Dillinger, his attorney] but, accentuating luck, he too could not be reached. He would not return from court until afternoon.

Authorities could not – would not? – await response, and the dread ritual was consummated. Once more I was handcuffed from behind and led toward the infamous 'Q' wing – horror house, where incorrigibles are kept and where society condones the frying of bodies with 2,000 volts of electricity.

I had an overwhelming urge to shout 'No' to this archaic, medieval madness. Breath quickened and step slowed.

But how could I fight? And whom? And what? Black male I am. From womb to hunger to ghetto, to arrest, jail, conviction and sentence of death – are they not all man-made graves? Are they not interchangeable?

Then why fight? Willingly I trod the corridor once more. Politely I thanked the assistant superintendent and headed to 'Q' wing. I knew immediately from the faces of the other prisoners that the pipeline had excelled as usual. Seemingly thousands of black faces reflected helplessness and hopelessness.

The 'girls' no longer called or threw kisses and propositions. They, as well, were truly concerned.

As prisoners, we are all seen by society as dirty things – untouchable, callous, violent. Yet murderers, rapists, thieves, and all manner of men from Pandora's Box stood silent, knowing the guards were carrying me off to be officially murdered. Bless them all – and yet I had a flicker of desire that they intervene. Quite the study of contrasts ...

We stopped briefly upon arrival at 'Q' wing. The guard tapped on a small plexiglass window. The door opened, and one of my escorts yelled, 'One for death watch.' The door slammed, was locked securely. Then – only then – did reality materialize.

Macabre ritual continued. Down flight of stairs (I am forever descending, always journeying, to life's pit).

And here I sit, stripped of property, gazing at bunk and pillow. Sheets and pillowcases are stamped in black: 'Death Watch'.

3.15 p.m.
I've not done much – unless staring at the ceiling counts. But finally speaking to my precious friend Marcia has washed away all fear. And she will also be visiting ...

4.30 p.m.
Against all will, sleep, visited ... I am miserable.

'Death Watch' is composed of six cells – three on the East side, three on the West, where I am located. The middle cell on each side is never occupied; it is used for clothing and linen storage.

Four of us currently await death in that inanimate object that is securely locked behind the door marked 'Exit'.

7.50 p.m.
'Doug, don't give up – for me, okay?' Katie McCray – my very all and everything, the precious human responsible for my existence. I curse myself for bestowing endless pain upon Mother – yet another innocent victim. She learned of my death warrant while at work. (Where else?) Yet she is confident matters will be fine ...

8.35 p.m.
The sergeant just made 'check', a progress repeated every fifteen minutes to assure one doesn't commit suicide. Death by execution, only. He will then log whatever I was doing at that particular moment.

8.40 p.m.
Epilepsy medication just arrived. The medical technician is accompanied by a shift lieutenant. His concern for my health will proceed until moment of death. The 'kindness' factor continues.

Saturday, May 28
3.00 a.m.
An all-white jury, serving as the voice of the community, heard the evidence against me, rejected death and voted for life imprisonment.

That being the case, why do I await death? God, why?

9.18 a.m.
Have I slept but two hours? Three? Four? One? Measuring time defies all reason, with so few dawns remaining ...

Life is stronger than all else – one chooses instinctively to inhale air until crushed by the hands of the state ...

The sergeant just passed for check. 'Everything OK McCray?' I nodded, tried to choke back the tears. I felt a compulsion to converse, to embrace him – I am in dire need of a soul to care ...

12.15 p.m.
Time – precious, oh, precious – passing immutably. I sit with my back to the door marked 'Exit', yet its presence is still felt. Its letters are badly printed in blood-red ink ... Some prisoner printed nervously. I am numb with fright, void of armor, ever aware of the wooden murderer looming mere feet away.

Beautiful day, this human Saturday. The highest and brightest of blue. Few clouds, many seagulls. And all tainted.

For nearly a decade I have searched diligently for the hidden asterisk to 'Thou Shalt Not Kill'. This is indeed the perfect crime. Because though I will be fried to death, no one will be held accountable. Courts, prosecutors, judges, jurors, prison officials all merely 'follow orders'. And the Governor – he will certainly acknowledge – is merely carrying out the will of the state.

And what of my executioner? The state will pay a citizen $150 to don a black hood and pull the switch. He will then – deed already forgotten – return to family and friends.

Sunday night, May 29
One seldom gets even a hello from guards. But God, they are talkative 'down here'. With sensibilities sharpened by knowledge of scheduled fate, guards become congenial and are helpful in obtaining legal materials and the like. And because they feel we will not escape death, they divulge many secrets ...

As I talked with a sergeant today, he pulled out a photo of himself, standing with a prized fish, beer in hand. 'Nice catch,' I said.

'I prayed for y'all in church.'

'I don't believe in that stuff,' replied Levi Aldrich. (He shares this side with me.)

'Are there any black members in your congregation?' I asked.

'No. But it's open to everybody.'

Monday, May 30
Another sour day, with morning passing quickly and my thinking of Mother's visit tomorrow.

A cleansing shower was utterly wonderful today. I was handcuffed behind my back, and three guards led me to the shower. The minute the cuffs were removed I paid very little attention to their constant stares. (They must watch; I must not attempt suicide.)

Evening
It is difficult to think rationally here. I have found relief from delirium by remembering those who share this dread as well. Family, friends and opponents of this medieval practice cling to hope of a stay of execution.

Don McCray, Death Row, Florida

Mercy's tea

The pecking orders, from church and states
With their holy water, and dinner dates
They've given the word, you are to expire
With infra red roses, wrapped in barbed wire
They're slaves to the thrill, with whiplash smiles
They've all lined up, in single file
They're here to watch, the seasonal trend
The stone reality, of one man's end
With cryptic lunches, pickled in glasses
They shut their doors, on opposing masses
With perfect lives, but fallen graces
We see their eyes, and heartless faces

The best of the cooked, and the best of the raw
Have cast their stones, down by the wall
It's pandemonium, no mercy's tea
Her potent levels, have ceased to be
But it will be quiet, before the storm
That stops your heart, for the norm
And feathers will fail, just like rain
As the angel of hearts, calls your name
There will be no prayers, this is true
By the severed souls, that are killing you
The dead letters office, of needles and rope
Has robbed society, of mercy's hope
They've left us bleeding, like Achilles' heel
Forget about them, they cannot feel
And angels' hair, will fall like snow
Soft on your shoulders, to let you know
You're not forgotten, you now are free
You're in the waters, of mercy's tea ...

Solemn words

Many acquaintances, and many good friends
Pay their respects, and their final amends
There's solemn faces, and there's watery eyes
They could be next, they've realized
The party has started, for the condemned man
Before his last walk, and final stand
There's a barrel of wine, like his maker's blood
Drank in good spirits, and in brotherly love
Counting the bricks, and the cracks on the floor
And remembering that face, behind the green door
Now 12.01 struck, the grim reaper's clock
And the hearts of the world, have all went in shock
The pellet has fallen, in the zyklon-5 pool
As our friend sits quietly on the cold stool
Waiting forever, is how it must seem
Thinking of life, as a dark dream
There's signs and protests, at the front gate
But as things look, I fear they're too late

And then the evening was clear, but a mite breezy
And seeing him go, was never said easy
And then morning came, and the party was over
The wind had died down, and the world was left sober
Not a roar of thunder, just acid rain
And the choking reminder, is what remained

Freedom at last

Praying for a chance, that will never come,
And watching your feelings grow hard, until they are
   numb.

Thinking of the days, before you were confined,
Whilst stuck in a cell, with limited time.

You flash on the memories, of a previous place,
And watching the years, put wear on your face.

You scream for Sweet Jesus, whilst hard on your
   knees,
With little or no chance, even as you breathe.

You've been slapped in the face, by the friends you
   once knew,
Not knowing why, not even a clue.

Your family sticks by you, when no one else will,
You wish you could change things, but time won't
   stand still.

You're a dead man tomorrow, that's how it all seems,
A memory of yesterday, and a life of pipe dreams.

It's hard to hang in there, with a rope over your head,
And no comforting spirits, from those who are dead.

You wait for the henchman, to pull your short straw,
And put you to sleep, for the good of them all.

But the wounds will stop hurting, from the pains of
    the past,
As you fall into the darkness, of freedom ... at last.

       Chris Tobin, Death Row, San Quentin, California

SONGS OF EXECUTION

At six o'clock we cleaned our cells,
  At seven all was still,
But the sough and swing of a mighty wing
  The prison seemed to fill,
For the Lord of Death with icy breath
  Had entered in to kill.

Oscar Wilde

Executions in the USA

I am in the middle, yet I am off to the side, waiting, watching while the state continues to set execution dates around me, so many dates I can't keep up with them. They have already carried out 7 executions here in Texas last year, 61 since they made Charlie Brooks the first to taste their poison in 1982, and if they have their way at least seven more will go before Xmas.

On May 3rd, 1993, Darryl Stewart became the 200th person executed in the US since the reinstatement of capital punishment, the 57th in Texas. On the eve of his execution I had a visit with a close friend. We sat in the visiting room looking at each other through the glass divider that separates loved ones from contact, talking through a double layer of security screen, trying to ignore the other people out there that had to visit their loved ones the same way. In the cage beside mine was Darryl Stewart. I did not know him, his name, his family, I did not even know he had a date set for that night. So many executions already, 10 times as many dates have been set, the news media as well as the people in here quit talking about the all too common, every day execution date a long time ago. So I sat there beside this man I didn't know, oblivious to the fact that he would be poisoned by the citizens of Texas in less than 12 hours. I saw his visitors, the kids crying, each of them taking turns walking away, trying to gather themselves before they sat back down. I have become calloused to the crying, I see it and hear it every time I have a visit, loved ones' hearts breaking, sensing that the living human being they know and love, the father, brother, son, husband, friend, will soon be poisoned, dead, murdered, gone.

Maybe I shouldn't say I am calloused to the crying, that sound of love that hurts so bad, because when I hear it I can feel it, even when I don't know who it is for. I think my heart and mind has just adapted – like society and the media has – because there is only so much pain a person can feel before the heart and mind shuts down and makes the pain go away.

I watched the guards – 'just doing my job' – come and tell him his visit was over, 'time's up' and then stand at the cage's door behind him. It was then that my visitor told me 'He has a date for tonight.' I looked back, the woman crying, the kids crying, him trying to say goodbye. Behind him the guards clicked their handcuffs open and shut, the metallic teeth clicking, clicking, clicking – 'just doing my job' – while they waited a moment before reaching into the 6" × 12" pan hole on the locked cage door and handcuffed him behind his back. The guards then took the padlock off of the cage door, opened it and escorted Darryl Stewart – the 200th person executed in the US since Gary Gilmore was shot in Utah, the 57th person poisoned in Texas – to a room out of sight so they could strip search him and then take him back to his cell to wait. His loved ones, still crying in the cold Ellis Unit visiting room after watching him walk away, put their arms around each other and walked away together.

With the area now quiet I looked at my friend and smiled an uncomfortable smile, both of us knowing this scene would be repeated again, and again, and again. Maybe me, maybe you.

Carlos Santana did it on the eve of 3/23/93; Ramon Montoya did it on the eve of 3/25/93; Leo Herrera on the eve of 5/12/93; John Sawyer on the eve of 5/18/93; Markum Duff-Smith on the eve of 6/28/93; and Curtis Harris on the eve of 7/1/93.

The day after they murdered Curtis Harris I was walking, handcuffed behind my back, down the main hall, coming from a visit with those precious thoughts and memories in my mind. Walking past one of the Death Row work program cell blocks, I heard a knock on the window and looked up to see Danny 'Rock' Harris waving at me. Trying to wave back, the handcuffs rattling, I once again felt that uncomfortable smile form on my lips. My heart hurt bad for Danny Harris, caught here on Death Row with the rest of us, unable to put his arms around the rest of his family while they cried over the loss of his brother.

New execution dates swirl round me like a Las Vegas roulette wheel, names and numbers coming to a stop, uncaring of the hearts that will break and the crying that will ensue. Maybe it is, after all, not me who is calloused. Maybe, maybe it is them.

To the loved ones, the families and friends of all who have been murdered. If life ever gets you down a bit, rest if you must but don't quit.

Robert West, Death Row, Huntsville, Texas

Death

is a morning song
morning sickness
a political act
who chooses to bury
a part of process
which feeds off life
what grief is myth
is dust to dust
the tears of snow
the clutching of a heart
dry squeezed
what are the lessons
you teach
are those scarred by
pain compatible
wandering dripping mourning
becomes what
a drunkenness
accursed unkind rogue
snatching words from
no!!
life alive can hear
a morning chirp.

Harold L. Otey, Death Row,
Nebraska State Penitentiary, Lincoln

Genocide in America

Oh, come now, how could that be happening? Is it some secret cult doing it? In this age of massive media coverage, any newsworthy story is milked to death. Surely, I would have heard about it if it were really happening. You have heard about it. You are told on a regular basis. But, in all fairness to you, it is camouflaged and fed to the public in a very palatable package. It is wrapped in a tasty cocoon of moral, religious and political sanctimonious justification, and it goes down pretty smooth. It is swallowed on a regular basis by a majority of the population of America. Because of the skillful justifications it is garnished with, it causes no mental or moral indigestion. So you can sleep at night secure in the knowledge that all is well. Those your government is killing deserve to die. You need no moral alka-seltzer for your conscience. Let's look behind the benevolent facade of this masterful presentation.

Like all propaganda, it creates moral indignation and inflames your sense of outrage. It takes a few of the most outrageous examples and through the media gives you a horror story and then whips your lust for revenge and retaliation to a frothing frenzy. This helps you accept all this government killing as justified and fair. If, at times, it gives you a moral problem or mentally tugs at your conscience, you simply recall the horror story you were told and your mind doesn't revolt. It becomes acceptable that we, as a society, commit murder to show that murder is wrong. Why does that statement seem so strange? Hard to think about and digest, isn't it? Because if you think about it, your next logical step is to reason that we are a society that has collectively lowered ourselves to the level of those we are so revolted by. We become murderers to prove murder is wrong. That's like saying if you rape my wife, I will come rape yours. If you molest my child, I will come molest yours. Whoa, now, this is getting way out of hand. No one could stomach that brand of retaliation. Well, that's exactly what we do about murder.

Today's executions you are never allowed to see. It's done by design, in a small secluded restricted place with only a few witnesses. You see, even the officials who kill for you know it's revolting. If ever exposed to the public, in a graphic videotape or national TV, the public would be sickened, shocked and totally disgusted. National support for this gruesome act would vanish.

In Georgia, they still electrocute you. You go through a full two minutes of electrical surges, alternating from super high surges in the thousands of volts, to a low of 1,200 volts – back and forth, up and down – coursing through your body continuously for the entire two minutes. Then they must wait a full six minutes before the medical doctor can take your pulse to officially declare you dead. Why wait six minutes? Is it to let your heart stop and give you time to die? No, it's for a far more practical reason than that. The six minute wait is so the doctor can stand to touch your skin to take your pulse. It takes six minutes for your well-done body to cool down enough to touch. You see, the full two minutes of alternating high voltage electrical surges literally cooks you from the inside out. You're electrically roasted.

One man in Alabama was hit with 1,900 volts. Sparks and flames shot from his head and leg area. White smoke visibly rose from under the death mask. He was examined and still alive, with a beating heart. They threw the switch again, sparks again flew from his head, and it literally burst into flames. Again, the doctors thought they felt a faint heartbeart. Incredibly, he was still alive after his head and leg had burst into flames twice. His attorney told the commissioner he would be charged with cruel and unusual punishment. This message was relayed to the governor. He ordered another jolt. I imagine this man in the chair, sitting there through all of this, with parts of his body cooked to the point of bursting into flames, still alive ... a third 1,900 volts was sent through his body. Mercifully, he finally died. The gut-wrenching stench of seared human flesh was incredibly strong. The warden explained, 'You're always going to have a smell of burnt human flesh – but not pain and suffering. You're gone immediately after the first jolt. There's not even a split second of recognition of what's happening to you.' I guess he has to tell himself that to stomach it. Must be nice to get into another human being ... and say with such certainty what's going on there. Tell that to the doctors and the man's family.

A former Alabama warden remembers a man they had to hit TEN times. Imagine the horror and stink of that person being fried.

A Georgia man didn't die after the first two minutes of surging electricity. He moaned and breathed deep breaths. Still, they waited six torturous minutes, even though they could see his chest visibly heaving with his breathing, fighting for life, before the doctor took his pulse and told them what they all had to know; that the struggling man was still very much alive. So they finally got him another two minute dose and killed him. Georgia uses higher voltage than Alabama. Where the leather straps touched his skin, small patches of skin and flesh stuck to the straps. The stench was overwhelming for twelve hours. These executions had to be terribly ugly. But, don't worry, you're insulated from the horror of it all.

Those same politicians who use crime as their primary platform and inflame your mind with horror stories, are the people who made the laws that enable the state to kill in your name, taking place in private restricted areas ... so, you can't see the ugliness of man and society at its depraved worst. If it's such a deterrent, put it on network TV and let the satellites beam it around the world.

Those sly politicians know that if it is unseen it's like it's not real to you. It's dreamlike and easier to dismiss. It's an unreal event, like a short, mildly unpleasant dream. It has no substance, no reality. It's been shrewdly minimized. Pretty crafty, really, those politicians are looking out for your conscience and sense of guilt. They are not about to lose or weaken such a productive platform and scare tactic. So, they can keep on killing in your name. A hidden sacrifice to the gods of revenge ... You wake up in the morning to coffee and toast and there may be a small news blurb that so-and-so was executed and the condemned went quietly. That's it, that's all you hear and read. That's all there is to it, to you. It went down easy with breakfast and you hardly noticed, if you noticed at all.

America is killing the economically deprived, those of the lower socio-economic strata, killing the insane, killing the retarded, killing illiterates, killing the emotionally crippled, killing the childishly immature and mentally undeveloped, killing the socially disenfranchised and the politically powerless of our society, killing those so criminally abused as children that they never had a chance to develop normally to a well-balanced human being. Their minds were stunted, twisted and mentally and emotionally destroyed as children.

We are killing the weaker of the species. We kill our mistakes. The financially strong and socially fortunate survive and the weak perish ... just like the jungle animal kingdom.

Wait a minute, we are a civilized society and this is not right. We have risen above the beasts of the jungle, haven't we? Well, that's what I am asking you, my reader. Have we truly risen above the jungle beasts?

Ronald Keith Spivey, Death Row, Jackson, Georgia

Silly questions

'How do you feel when one of you are
 killed?'
I'm often asked by those off the row.
And when I reply I usually lie
Because somehow they can never know.

How do you say, 'I silently scream,
Feel volatile and want to hide'?
That their question is intrusive, any
Answer illusive, and impinges on your
pride.

Ask why it's right they kill in the night
If their deeds are as bright as the day.
Or why justice so blind, it kills humankind
Is called anything but gray.

Well, I think they're thrilled when we're
 killed.

I can answer those questions in haste.
But if you're a friend, don't ask again,
Because the answer's reflected in your face

Thomas Battle, Missouri

Condemned

i sit here a condemned person
it does not matter which gender
i am i am doomed
i must die to atone for
your fears to purge your hearts
of guilt at not being almighty
all over-protective omnipresent
to be everywhere to stop all
hurt all pain all crime
all of the many
me in plurality 3-D you hate
are afraid to ask me
why
dare not find out that
i am i am no different than
the person you see on the
street or in the bus or at
work or in the church or wearing
the uniform of every day
you dare not love
because
then it would be us
this we
who struggle to understand
why must there be
this excuse for killing
be i gay in the military
or woman independent aggressive
or black chinese arabic hispanic
manchild in your land
i must die

because i see i talk i feel
unlike you mine was
with only a plea for
forgiveness
image only an attitude
and life alive a humanism
mistakes made
true gods do not fear
mere people locked away do.

Harold L. Otey, Death Row,
Nebraska State Penitentiary, Lincoln

Executions are degrading to society

'When we abolished the punishment for treason that you should be hanged and then cut down while still alive, then disembowelled while still alive, and then quartered, we did not abolish that punishment because we sympathized with traitors, but because we took the view that this was a punishment no longer consistent with our self-respect.' These words, spoken by Lord Chancellor Gardiner during the 1965 death penalty abolition debates in the British Parliament, illustrate the feeling felt by most individuals opposed to capital punishment. It's not sympathy towards the murderer that we feel, indeed most of us feel a great deal of anger and revulsion towards him and his actions. Our objection is that it is a complete renunciation of all that is embodied in our concept of humanity. Or simply put, executions degrade us all.

In today's society, the execution process is far removed from most individual citizens. We may be aware of the criminal acts that put an individual on Death Row – usually through sensationalized press accounts – but very few of us know of the human being who society has condemned to death. And even fewer of us have ever witnessed, or ever will witness, an actual execution. This dehumanization of the whole process makes it easy for us to distance ourselves from capital punishment and accept it 'as something government does', allowing us not to be responsible for the consequences of such actions.

We need to be aware of the human side of executions. Therefore, I'd like to share with you an extract from an affidavit by David Bruck, an attorney, who stayed with a condemned man, Terry Roach, during the last hours before his execution.

'I assisted with Terry Roach's defense during the last month before his execution, and I spent the last four hours with Terry Roach in his cell when he was electrocuted on January 10, 1986.

Although I have known Terry slightly for several years, meeting him in the course of visits to see other inmates on South Carolina's Death Row, my first long conversation with Terry occurred less than a month before his death. An execution date had already been set, and he seemed frightened and very nervous. I was struck at that time by how obviously mentally retarded Terry was ... I had known from following his case through the courts that he had been diagnosed as mildly mentally retarded, but I was still surprised at his slack-jawed and slow way of speaking, and at the evident lack of understanding of much of what we were telling him about the efforts that were underway to persuade Governor Riley to grant clemency.

The next time that I would see Terry was on the night of his execution. The lawyers who had worked on his case for the past eight years were at the Supreme Court in Washington, so I had decided to look in on Terry that night after his family had to leave for the last time, to see if I could help him with anything or just keep him company. When I arrived, he had decided to ask me to stay with him through the night and to accompany him when he was taken to the chair. So along with Marie Deans, a paralegal and counselor who works with condemned prisoners in Virginia, I stayed.

Although Terry was twenty-five years old by the time of his death, he seemed very childlike. In general, his demeanor and his reactions to the people around him appeared to me to comport with the finding, made at his last psychological evaluation, that his IQ was 70 – a score which placed his intellectual functioning at about the level of a twelve-year-old child. When his family minister showed him some prayers from the Bible that they would read together, Terry asked him which ones he thought would be especially likely to help him into heaven: his questions about this seemed based on the childish assumption that one prayer was likely to "work" better than another, and that he just needed some advice about which ones would work best. Later in the night, he asked me to read him a long letter about reincarnation that a man from California had sent to him just that day: he listened to the letter with wonder, like a small child at bedtime, trusting and uncritical. Both Marie and I were struck by how calmed Terry seemed by the sound of a voice reading to him in the resonant cell, and we spent much of the remaining time reading to him while he listened, gazing at the reader with rapt attention.

He had a final statement which his girlfriend had helped him write. When I arrived that night, the statement was on three small scraps of paper, in his girlfriend's handwriting. I copied it out for him, and got him to read it out loud a few times. No matter how many times he tried, the word "enemies" came out "emenies". He kept practicing it, but pronouncing the written word just seemed beyond his capabilities. Still, he seemed to like the rehearsal: like everything we did that night, it filled the time and acknowledged that he was doing something very difficult.

Terry was a very passive young man, and that showed all through the night. Although he was obviously frightened, he was as co-operative as possible with the guards, and he tried to pretend that all the ritual preparation – the shaving of his head and right leg, the prolonged rubbing in of electrical conducting gel – was all a normal sort of thing to have happen. He wanted the approval of those around him, and he seemed well aware that this night he could gain everyone's approval by being brave and keeping his fear at bay.

Still, when the warden appeared in the cell door at 5.00 a.m. and read the death warrant, while Terry stood, each wrist immobilized in a manacle known as the "claw", his left leg began to shake in large, involuntary movements. After that everything happened quickly. I walked to the chair with him, and talked to him as much as I could. He wanted me to read his statement, but I told him that he ought to try and I'd read it if he couldn't. His voice was only a little shaky, and he managed quite well, except for "emenies". After he had repeated the name of a friend of mine who had recently died, and whom he had offered to look up for me when he got to heaven, I left him and walked to the witness area, where I gave him a "thumbs-up" sign. He signalled back with his fingers, as much as the straps permitted. We signalled to each other once more just before the mask was pulled down over his face.

A few seconds later the current hit. Terry's body snapped back and held frozen for the whole time that the current ran through his body. After a few seconds, steam began to rise from his body, and the skin on his thigh just above the electrode began to distend and blister. His fists were clenched and very white. His body slumped when the power was turned off, and jerked erect again when it was resumed. When he was declared dead, several guards wrestled his body out of the chair and onto a stretcher, while taking care to conceal his face (no longer covered by the mask) from the view of the witnesses and me by covering it with a sheet. I left the death house at about this time in the company of the warden. As we stepped out of the building, I heard the whoops of a crowd of about 150 or 200 demonstrators who had apparently come to celebrate the execution, and who were yelling and cheering outside the prison gates.'

Executions degrade us all. They are held in the middle of the night, in the dark, away from us all, to hide what they really are. The men who are condemned to death are dehumanized by the state and by the press, to make it easier to carry out their executions. And the public is kept as far away as possible from the whole process to keep them from seeing that human beings, real flesh and blood, real people, are being put to death. That is the only way that any state or government can continue executions without the public demanding its eradication.

It's time for us to acknowledge capital punishment for what it really is, and to abolish it nationwide. There are suitable alternatives, for example, in my state those convicted of capital crimes, who are not sentenced to death, are sentenced to life imprisonment *without possibility of release.* This is clearly a suitable alternative to executions, and satisfies society's need to be protected from dangerous individuals. It is not necessary to kill criminals, not even the most reprehensible ones, and to continue to do so truly lowers us to the level of the very ones that we wish to punish. And undoubtedly degrades us all.

Michael Ross, Death Row, Somers, Connecticut

Death on the wind

People kill things every day
From love to idle time
And some things die anyway
From life to idle minds.

It couldn't really hurt to die
No more than it hurts to live
The people left always cry
When there's nothing left to give.

Death is just the final sleep
As dust to dirt we go
In little piles that dirt we sweep
As the wind outside still blows.

And the wind kills time itself
It eats away this earth
And everything once known as wealth
The wind will turn to dirt.

To know death is to know the wind
That whispers through the trees
And death is just another friend
Blowing on the breeze.

Thomas E. Creech, Death Row, Idaho

An Award of Merit Certificate from the World of Poetry, Sacramento, was awarded to Thomas E. Creech for this poem.

Executioner

The shadow of death may walk on feet of air
... but his name I know;

It is so much his custom to steal in the night,
Or creep thru' day's shadows
Disguised as a thief;
... but his name I know.

One may ponder the ages
How this shadow of death may introduce himself,
And never expect the obvious;
... because his name you know!

We have shaken hands, death's shadow and I,
Twice in as many years ...
But never an ubiquitous clinch
... for I truly know his name.

With a deep, faint gleam of yearning
In the dark recesses of my eyes
... I laughed!

For not only do I know his name,
I have learned his mode as well;
And when he comes, that third and final time
... I will embrace him ...
The surprise will be his,
... for then he will surely know my name!

James Armando Card, Snr, Death Row,
Florida State Prison, Starke

Final hour
(for Robert Harris who was executed
in California in 1992)

He walked down the tier
with his head held high,

And stopped at each cell
to say his last goodbye.

Five hours were left
on his final day,
Then the court came through
with a seven day stay.

A preacher man on TV
said he should die slow,
Is this preacher man any different
than us on Death Row?

In front of the cameras
he stood ready and willing,
To cheer for the state
when they started their killing.

This preacher seemed happy
to see Harris die,
He quoted from the Bible
'an eye for an eye'.

If an eye for an eye
was the law of the land,
Then the world would be blind
including you, preacher man.

Ray 'Running Bear' Allen, Death Row,
San Quentin, California

Death by injection

Gruff manner, stoic faces, and strong hands about me,
Hold me ready for the ordeal,
Pushing me to and fro,
Guiding me across the floor.

Sweeping me from perpendicular,
Quick movement, bright lights,
Harnessed horizontal,
Straps bind me, snug and tight.

One arm out and held tightly bound,
A sting and poke, skin pierced,
A look of vengeance around,
Sterile needle stuck and taped.

Quick gaze about,
Faces suddenly appear,
A final shout,
Witnesses come to see and hear.

Tubes snake into the beyond,
Moving rapidly along,
The first drug makes me yawn,
Images fade, nausea ...

Bile has no time to arise,
The heart stopper,
Is sent to paralyze,
It is over.

Quickly, quickly, quickly,
They move to sanitize,
Sickly, sickly, sickly,
Brutalize and humanize?

Steven King Ainsworth, Death Row, San Quentin, California

Defiance

The juggernaut, foreboding and large, travels toward its
     prey,
Stopping not for funeral pyres, nor heeding deathbed pleas.

Wingbeats of rancid breath print lightly on my skin,
Panting like a winded dog, I urge my feet to keep the pace.
I am chased throughout the night, with only dew to
    quench my thirst;
To falter would invite the end, and close all windows in my
    face.

(Spirit, say a prayer for me and bring my wonders home to
    thee!)

Innocence, once my cloak of faith, is but a saddened
    picture now,
A mere reminiscence coddled by the denigration of a
    hungry soul.
Somewhere – perhaps in an ogre's teeth – my deepest
    heart lies captured.
Beyond my reach it shouts to me, but, alas, its voice is
    weak and cracked.
Forgive me Father, for I have sinned; I cringed away from
    Fate –
Cowardice turned me strikingly with a promise of better
    days.

(Spirit, say a prayer for me and bring my wonders home to
    thee!)

I cry, I cry, I cry for love, but deafness overtakes me.
The juggernaut, steadfast and sure, bears down on Hellish
    feet.
Of what purpose has my lifetime been if not to tell the tale?
Would those who dare to follow me not care to know the
    truth?
Reflected in my moonlit shadow, a simple man sprints
    onward;
With legs aflame like comet tails, he leaves the Beast in
    dust.

Geno, Death Row, Huntsville, Texas

The lion

The show was over, he packed it in
The people came, with faces grim
He bought the bullet, a one way ticket
The signs were up, they came to picket
The lion knew, it was the end
But he ate his meal, alone in the den
Newsmen wrote, newsmen lied
And said farewell, as they ran to hide
He seen the traffic, he seen the life
He seen the terror, he seen the knife
He smelled the flesh, and the bone
But could not tell, it was his own
And so he stood, white and tall
As he slowly, came to fall
For all to see, for all to hear
For all to wonder, for all to fear
No tears had fell, no words were said
No one cared, that the lion was dead

Chris Tobin, Death Row, San Quentin, California

Conversations with the dead

'These are the graves of the executed ones,'
he announced with a somber, indifferent kind of
   respect ...
and yet later, in quiet reflection,
I understood his tone came up out of
that secret reservoir of the soul which knows
'I, too, could end up as forgotten dust;
I, too, might die for nothing.'

Often now I think back upon my journey
through that phantom land: a land caught
like evening haze at dusk, soon to perish
into the gathering darkness of night
but, for one brief moment, beyond time.

I recall its mute, mouthless people,
inhabitants of a dark land whose hopeless,
dying eyes gazed dully at my passage
from their skullish heads. They saw me
only as a traveler who wanted nothing
and took nothing from them. They knew only
that they were not harmed.

I remember the aura which lay like heavy
blankets over that tortured land, an aura
of scarred spirits vanquished by the
horrible vendetta of an angry god.

I remember the excited buzz of feasting flies
as they drank still-warm blood, ate the still-quivering
flesh, and lustfully gorged themselves
on all the disappointments man can devise.

I remember, as if it were now, the picture
of a burned statue of the Virgin Mary
and the image of a small child kneeling
in prayer before it, weeping for a murdered mother
whose name, also, was Mary.

I recall those I, too, have slain:
those by my wrath seized, stolen from life,
becoming but candles lit by children
who became adults before childhood lived.
I recall their dying, their sparks fading,
gone like that: out. Returned to the void.
Nothing.

'These are the executed ones,' he said.
I recall standing there alone, filled
by the putrid odor of stinking jungles,
sunscorched deserts, savage streets,
knowing the drowning sensation of my own
awakening, pulling me down into the swirling
cauldron of enlightenment.

I recall how a warm wind brushed my face
and then was gone. I remember touching
a grim stone, experiencing how that dust
had lived: born of anguish to laugh,
make love, and perhaps do it again tomorrow
until at last death came,
speaking of one other place to be
consumed by life: that stopping place
where I, too, found these things.

'These are the executed ones,' he stated, eyes
small sparks, and then was gone, dissolving
into the umbra arts of night,
leaving but those sparks which smolder in my soul,
like candles surrounding the powerless and
charred Virgin's image in a chapel.
'These are the executed ones,' he announced,
studying a horizon of tombstones. 'Pray for them ...
and for those to come.'

Stephen Wayne Anderson, Death Row,
San Quentin, California

THE ART OF LOSING: BEREAVEMENT

The art of losing isn't hard to master.

Elizabeth Bishop

But there is no sleep when men must weep
  Who never yet have wept:
So we – the fool, the fraud, the knave –
  That endless vigil kept,
And through each brain on hands of pain
  Another's terror crept.

Oscar Wilde

A priceless gift

On the day we heard Billy's news I was training a group of newly redundant people in the complexities of finding a new job. The phone rang; Mary's voice was unusually distant. She said, 'Billy's going to die on April 23rd.' With his letter to us was the District Judge's order – it was cold, clinical and had been sent to him through the mail.

When I put the phone down, one of the group said, 'Are you OK, Tim?' Like Mary, I was shaken. In a previous letter, we had joshed with Billy because he had signed himself, 'Your son, Billy'. To have reached that sort of rapport with another human being is privilege enough, but we look upon ourselves as being blessed by his presence in our lives. Now, suddenly, it was all going to be pulled away from us.

I asked the group for a few minutes and I walked into the gardens around our offices, trying to bring a whole range of conflicting emotions under control in the spring sunshine. There was anger at the premeditated ritual, fear for someone who was all alone and who we both love as a delightful and, yes, decent human being who had screwed up as a youth all those years ago, and there was also gratitude for having him in our lives.

Thankfully we visited Billy in Huntsville in October last year. He was tall, black and handsome in his white prison fatigues; a gentle, slow man (the papers said he was retarded), softly spoken. He smiled a lot. We drew very close to this man who had not seen or heard from his family in years and we became – as are we all with our correspondents – his eyes and ears on the outside world. He responded to our descriptions of walks by telling us of the cloudscapes and birds he saw beyond the razor wire outside his cell window. He told us how he missed walking on grass and how he would have loved to have stroked our cats.

Two weeks before he was killed, we sent Billy our last letter. It was composed to bring him comfort and to reinforce our love for him. It never reached him. It was returned with 'Deceased' written across the envelope.

As far as we know, Billy died alone – no family, no friends. Was he able to hug the granny who raised him? The papers said that he had helped the officials to find a vein for the injection. He was on the gurney for 47 minutes, the last nine of which it took him to die. Billy is gone and our lives are emptier than before. He gave us so much happiness. A week after his execution an envelope from him arrived. In it was a linen handkerchief. There is a poem on it, typed and with spelling errors. I think it sums up what we offer our correspondents. It certainly summed up our friendship with Billy:

> Friendship is a promise spoken only
> by the heart.
> It isn't given by any pledge.
> It isn't written on any paper.
> It's a promise to share sad and glad
> times.
> A promise to think of each other
> fondly whether near or far apart.
> Friendship is a priceless gift that
> can't be bought or sold.
> But to have an understanding friend
> is worth far more than gold.
> A friend is there before you know it,
> to lend a hand,
> Before you ask, and give you love
> just when you need it most

REST IN PEACE MY FRIEND

Tim Binder, LifeLines

I must not fear

Dear Tim and Mary,

I hope that this letter finds the both of you in the very best of God's loving care. As for myself, the tension has been eased a bit thanks to the both of you. As to what would have happened had you not been there for me, I'm scared to think about it and it's really hard for me to say. Really only God knows the true answer to that question.

And you are right about our justice system – it actually operates in favor of the rich, and the poor suffer. The whole process basically starts over once the stay is granted. So to tell you both without you I would probably be real bad off right about now and I love you both for the support and true concern for my well being.

When you speak of us growing up in the middle of the family you couldn't have said it any better.

I'm delighted to know that someone is making an effort to end this journey of assassination here in Texas, because this is totally beyond the element of murder. Please always remember it's people like you that makes a difference in this world.

I also feel it's a great honor to be referred to as your son instead of just a friend. Our relationship has risen above and beyond what I could have ever imagined, and that's one thing I will never regret no matter what happens.

Mary I haven't forgotten about your birthday. They just don't have the right kind of cards for you, so don't be stunned because it's late. I truly wish I could have been there for her on that wonderful day, but hopefully I will make many others (smile).

I hope and pray by the time my next letter reaches you, I will have gotten a stay from the courts. It shouldn't be too long before I hear something, but as I said you will be the first to know and that's a fact.

Well I guess I better close this letter for now, and once again thanks for all the help and love you have shown me, which is something I never thought truly existed. May God bless and keep the both of you in good care. You're in my every thoughts and prayers. I love the both of you very much!

Love always, Billy

> I must not fear
> Fear is the mind-killer
> Fear is the little death
> That brings total obliteration
> I will face my fear

I will permit it to pass over me
And through me
And when it has gone past
I will turn the inner eye
To see its path
Where the fear has gone
There will be nothing
Only I remain

(I hope that you like it)

Billy Wayne White

Billy Wayne White was executed by the state of Texas in April 1992.

The last letter

Dear Billy,

Thanks Buddy for your last letter to us. We are both glad that the money reached you and that your papers have been filed for a stay. I guess that by the time you receive this letter you will know one way or the other how successful the application has been. If it has been successful then that is wonderful news – if not then ... well I guess that is what this letter is about. We both want you to know how we feel about you and hopefully there will be some lines of comfort for you.

Firstly Billy, you need to know and remember that you have brought a wonderful joy into our lives. If anyone ever believes that people behind bars are cut off from doing any good, we know better. Your letters from that place are treasures to us and the love that they carry is something that nothing can ever take away from us. The sort of relationship that we have built up is one that is built upon trust and respect on both sides – and you can't have real deep love for another person without having those two. It's also something that transcends color, race, creed and political beliefs. When we write to 'our Billy' it is not a black inmate that we write to – it is a person, another human being who (let's not beat around the bush) screwed up as a young guy – but who has got wonderful reserves of love that we are privileged to have him share with us. He is a person, a real, living, breathing person whose feelings and emotions are like any other's. And above all he is a person who is part of our lives, who we are proud of and who we are happy to refer to as 'our Son'. That's not bad going from a few letters, is it?

You know, Billy, another thing has happened. Our concern for you has spread to many, many others. All of our families and friends know of and about you and they always ask, 'Is Billy OK?' There are a lot of minds all sending you loving thoughts.

Let's get to the difficult bit – those things that could happen in less than a couple of weeks. Firstly Billy, you need to know where I am coming from when I talk about death and dying. My overwhelming belief is in a truly loving God (I use the words like Infinite Love and Goodness and Divine Lifeforce and Intelligence as well as God, but they all mean the same thing to me) whose Creation is all around us (and that includes us too) and who holds this Creation together in love and harmony. I do not see an old man sitting on a cloud dispensing judgement and being nasty to 'sinners'. No I see the purest Love imaginable, that is as close to you and me and everyone and everything else, as the next breath we take and as far away as the farthest galaxy in the unending universe. This Love is also in the atoms and cells that make up our bodies and in all the atoms and molecules everywhere. This Infinite Love is everywhere all the time – we are never separated from it for one second – and this means to me that no matter what happens to us we are in the end safe. This also means that the life force that flows through you is the same one that flows through me, through Mary, and through every flower, bird, creature and star. I am sure that deep down you probably already are aware of this.

Your little poem was good, Billy. You have managed to put into a few words what it would take a psychologist hundreds of pages to describe – but then we always knew that there was something special about you. Please let us have any other poems you have written – we would treasure them like we do your letters.

We've had some fine weather recently and we spent a bit of time in the garden – the spring flowers are out now and the new leaves look young and softly green – strange isn't it, how during the winter everything looked dead and now it is all clothed in new life? We sat on a log and looked out over the water from which the sunlight glanced and glinted, and said, as we often do, 'Billy would love it here.' We also had a letter from a friend who wrote 'If Texas doesn't want Billy, let them send him over here, we'll look after him' – we have to agree with that!

Mary just reminded me that when she was very young, just after World War Two, she had two cats at her grandmother's called Peter and Billy. Peter was always scratching her but Billy was a big, gentle and loving black cat who meant the world to her and gave her a lot of love. Somewhere along the line there is a link here!

So dear Billy, we don't know how this will find you. Maybe the stay has been successful, maybe not – but it has given us the chance to talk about a subject that we would normally skate around. Our relationship has now been cranked up another notch.

Whatever happens, you are held closely in the arms of our thoughts and we love you. If the worst does happen we know you will be brave. You can try to hold on to the good, love and joy that you have given to us and know that your time here has not been wasted. We will watch your ship sail over the horizon – you will then be able to watch out for ours arriving when the time comes.

Be brave son, be strong and never forget that you are loved by us and many others, now and always.

Tim and Mary

This was the letter that never reached Billy, even though it was sent to him well before his execution. It was returned marked 'Deceased'. The following letter was written by Billy's cell mate.

Mourning on the Row

My dearest Tim and Mary,

I hope this letter finds you in the best of God's Loving Care, and I also pray it will bring the two of you wonderful people a peace in mind.

My name is Odell Barnes Jr and I am here on Death Row in Texas. I live in 213 cell. Yes, I was Billy's neighbor and more like his Little Brother. I looked to him as the Big Brother I never had. Prior to the murder of my Big Brother, he asked me 'If worse comes to worse will you write Tim and Mary and tell them what I'm about to tell you?' I told Bill, 'Man, think positive you aren't going nowhere.' He told me, 'Just promise you will.' So I promised him! Well he gave me your address, but I didn't write it down. Then they moved him to Death Watch, he sent me a message and told me 'I love you, Little Brother.' Yes, my heart sank to the deepest level because he had told me I would know if he was taken to be executed and I knew. At 12.49 a.m. he was given the needle and at 12.58 a.m. my Dear Brother was with God.

Now I will fulfill the wishes of my dear friend, so here goes. Bill told me to tell the both of you that he never doubted your love for him, and not to feel as though you had failed him, you were the mother and father he never really had, and to tell you that was the greatest thing he felt you should know. As for the money you were able to send him gave him at least a few more minutes of life and he loved you for all the understanding and support, and must I say to know people out there do actually care makes a difference and *I thank you* for at least giving him some security and sense of being a human once again. Bill talked about the two of you endlessly, he was proud of the love you showed him and he told me he didn't know where his mind would be if you two were not there to find a loving hand, and he wanted you to know that the hand you gave and the love you showed was well spent, and he told me to stress this point clearly.

Tim and Mary, Billy told me to tell you *don't give up on the cause* and to find another fellow inmate here who also needs the same love that you showed him, but most of all *don't give up*; he didn't give up my friends, he was senselessly murdered and this is why we must continue to Fight for Life and Stop the Killing.

I want to thank you for the love, care and understanding you showed my dear friend. But I feel he is happier now with God, because if he couldn't have freedom, then I'd rather see heaven because this place is truly Satan's house and Bill felt the same way until you came into his life. So be proud, you both are special and remember you *did make a difference* regardless of the outcome.

Once again, I love and thank the both of you for your love for Billy and being the parents he never had.

And on behalf of my Beloved Brother I send love and hope for a better world.

May God bless you dear loving people, because without love there is no kind of hope, and without you hope is dead. I love you both and I pray for your well being. Goodbye my friends.

Sincerely,
Your friend, Odell Barnes Jr

A strong spirit

Not always right or wrong,
But strong.
A sincere smile,
Even if he was a little wild.
The strength of 'Still Bill'
Will never be killed.
Although his body is gone,
His spirit is still strong.
He could express laughter and joy,
Even though he was sometimes treated as a toy.
They played with his life until the end;
These foolish, simple, silly men.
But a strong spirit will never end,
'Still Bill's' strength will not bend.

Until the end of time,
His spirit will shine;
Because 'a strong spirit' was his kind!

(Dedicated to Billy 'Still Bill' White. A brother, a son, a father, a friend; executed in Texas on April 23, 1992.)

Ronald K. Allridge, Death Row, Huntsville, Texas

A thought for a friend
25 September 1991

A man died today. A man who was loyal, decent and full of humility. This man was my friend. A friend whose love of living and humour was matched by his courage and willingness to fight in his own quiet, peaceful way. Very few of us know when we are to die. My friend did. In normal circumstances such knowledge is the passport to making the most of the remaining time. My friend did not have that luxury, although within the confines of the shackles that held him, he travelled far and knew more about life and about living than any of us ever will.

My friend died with no anger inside him. No taunts of revenge or beyond-the-grave retribution came from his lips. Perhaps I can learn from him, because I am ready to explode with anger, pain and hatred against those who have murdered him. One day, yes, one day, his killers will have to look God in the face. And me. I don't know who they should fear the most – but I have an idea!

Of course, the fight against the death penalty is bigger than one man's death. I urge everyone involved to try just a little bit harder. Warren McCleskey's death must not be in vain. We must fight for everything that he so passionately believed in. He's somewhere now, smiling at this fool who is trying to write some sense, fighting the endless tears that are falling onto this keyboard.

The world is a poorer place since you left it, Warren. They broke your grip on life, but they did not break your spirit. In time, the many shall not remember. I shall never forget you. Rest in peace, my friend.

WARREN McCLESKEY 1945–1991

Mark Penn

Mark Penn is a LifeLiner who inaugurated the Warren McCleskey award.

The art of losing

Living on Death Row in America, how does one put this lifestyle into words? How can a person who has not lived this life possibly understand the impact this life has on a prisoner? Only through the prisoner's words, thoughts and ideas will you receive some type of a description of life on Death Row, and even this will never give you a complete picture. The hardest part of living this life is waking each day knowing that you have been sent here to be killed. Most of us here have gotten on with our life in search of a life that we can claim as our own, others have set out to find ways to bring this lifestyle to an end, suicide and legal victories, or just plain letting go of reality.

When I first arrived on Death Row, I saw little hope in my future or within myself, but over the years I have been able to change that about myself. Anger towards the system has given me the strength to fight the very idea that these people who control my every move are actually here to take from me the one thing they haven't the right to take from me, my life.

I have seen the Beast take the lives of three men in one year's time. The last man they killed was a picture perfect example of a man rehabilitated, not only by the system of course, as the system has no rehabilitation programme for Death Row prisoners, their logic being that our rehabilitation will come with death. No, this man rehabilitated himself out of his own desire to be a better man for those he loved and cared for. Had the system allowed this man to continue on with life, I am certain this man would still be pushing himself to become an even better person than he was when the system killed him.

The judicial system said that this man must be put to death in order to rid society of a danger, to preserve justice. Well the system carried out this nation's idea of justice, and in doing so they have placed upon the family and friends of this man an injustice.

The family of this man has been given a life sentence of their own, one that they now must serve, thrown into their own private prisons without ever breaking the law. Yes the Beast has grabbed another life, and with each life this Beast takes, many more lives are destroyed ...

Daniel W. Cook, Death Row, Arizona State Prison, Florence

Written in memory of James Dean Clark, executed on 14 April 1993.

Come back to me

Today I thought to myself
Today I fought with myself
Come back to me, come back to me
My love I once had
Come back to me, come back to me
My peace I'll be glad
Today I cry by myself
Someday I'll die by myself
Come back to me, come back to me
My spirit I'm sad
Come back to me, come back to me
My life I'll be glad
Today I must say to myself
Today I must pray for myself
Oh God! my love from heaven above
Oh God! my peace, which never cease
Oh God! my spirit, I pray you hear it
Oh God! my life, my life, my life

Keith B. Taylor, Death Row, Jackson, Georgia

RELEASE

For his departure, arrangements had been made so that he would not find himself being stared at as he had been at Clapham Junction on his transfer to Reading [prison]. He was allowed to wear ordinary clothes and was not handcuffed ... Two reporters had come to observe his departure, and to one of them he said, as quoted in the *New York Times*, that he 'coveted neither notoriety nor oblivion'. Then he and two prison officials took a cab to Twyford station. Wilde almost gave the game away when he opened his arms towards some budding bush saying, 'Oh beautiful world! Oh beautiful world!' The warder implored him to stop. 'Now, Mr Wilde, you must not give yourself away like that. You're the only man in England who would talk like that in a railway station.'

Richard Ellmann in his biography of Oscar Wilde

Yet all is well; he has but passed
   To Life's appointed bourne:
And alien tears will fill for him
   Pity's long-broken urn,
For his mourners will be outcast men,
   And outcasts always mourn.

Oscar Wilde

When I think of you

yesterday i could only think
some day soon this all will end
the pain the anguish the aloneness
oh so much frustration read in the faces of
those who do not fathom the beauty of living
its shortness here on earth and us
why we are the way we hug cry want desire
each other but a battered being sagging
beneath the infinity of time i wanted
them to know as i did we can take none of
this as ours but should camp out under the stars
which bless and glimmer our hopes if only
for a tomorrow i could think that
knowledge must indeed rise up so
that all can see and learn grasp and enjoy
for where else could it stay but in the heavens
out beyond our reach but close enough to want
because we know it is there and find it
indescribable as is the warmth of home.

Harold L. Otey, Death Row,
Nebraska State Penitentiary, Lincoln

Pale guano

Clank! Clank! Clank! The sound of the keyman unlocking the cell doors echoed through the cell block. Clank! Clank! Clank! He moved at a steady pace down the tier marking the rhythm of the cell block's 6.00 a.m. awakening.

Throwing my bed covers back I rolled out of my hard prison bed, the cold cement floor making me walk on the sides of my feet as I hurriedly staggered to the sink. Quickly hitting the cold water button I splashed my face, washing the sleep from my eyes. Groping around for a towel, I found it and wiped my face dry.

Jamming a rolled-up *National Geographic* magazine between the sink's edge and the hot water button I let the

*Steven King
Ainsworth, Death Row,
San Quentin,
California*

water run, hoping it would be especially hot this morning. Collecting my clothes I quickly dressed, stripped my bed, and folded up the thin mattress. Then I filled by plastic tumbler with hot water and spooned in my last bit of instant coffee.

Sipping the rich mixture I sat down on the steel bed and listened to the clank! clank! of the keyman unlocking the cells, the hot water running in the sink, and the myriad sounds of convicts waking up with the disappointment that their dreams lied to them and they were still in the cell that they had fallen asleep in the night before.

Clank! Clank! Clank! The sound was getting closer. The keyman stopped at my door.

'Today?' he asked.

'Yeah, man, today,' I answered.

'Good luck,' he said, moving on with his keys and clanking sound.

'Thanks,' I replied, moving over to the sink and turning off the hot water. Taking my pass to freedom off the shelf above the sink I read it for the umpteenth time.

'R & R 8.30 a.m.' I was being released today after five long years.

'6.00 a.m. unlock,' the public address system blared. The security bar slid back to free the cell doors and I pushed mine open and kicked my bedding out on the tier. I stepped out of my cell with my shoe box of personal belongings, not much for five years, even though I started with less.

Moving off towards the main cell block doors I looked about for a sign that this indeed would be my last exit, but all I saw was the angry scowls of the men about me, a reminder of the years I had wasted in this pit.

Stepping out of the cell block into the dewy air, a light fog obscured some of the details, but you knew that the armed guards were alert on the gunrails overhead, the snouts of their weapons pointing down with deadly menace.

We marched with shuffling feet towards the big dining hall with its murals depicting progress and discovery. The chow line formed along this wall, each convict's back tight against it as he slid along towards the steam table and its bounty of felon fodder.

Rubbery green scrambled, powdered eggs, sided with hard nuggets of reconstituted dehydrated potatoes, a generous portion of stewed prunes to ease the passage, topped off with a carton of milk that tasted like fermented silage and a cup of ersatz coffee rounded out the morning repast.

Glumly, I held out my tray as the server flopped my issue of each on it. Moving along I found an empty spot at one of the tables and sat down with three others. Warily looking at one another and none of us saying anything, we quickly gulped the mess before us, each hoping that we would finish eating before a fight or riot broke out. Visions of hard-edged trays flying around, utensils thrown, and bullets ricocheting endlessly around the cement walls as the gun guards fired mercilessly with glee to end the melee hurried each spoonful to our mouths.

Finishing, we each rose and left the mess hall, me with my little shoe box under my arm. I wandered down under the big metal shed that covered the upper yard area where the white boys had staked out their territory.

No matter where you went in prison each ethnic group had their particular spot to stand. Seldom did the groups integrate until the crowd of convicts got so large that the different groups were forced into proximity of each other. Even then there remained a distinct body-wide line of demarcation around each group.

Some convicts I knew from each group exchanged veiled signs of recognition. I cupped my pass in my hand and waved at each, making little walking-man signs with my fingers. Some caught it and gave me the A-okay of circled fingers and thumb. Others just looked and gave one finger, the middle one, straight up!

I looked up, the shed roof peppered with bullet holes and the girders lined with the ever-present pigeons. Moving over behind the shed I looked up to the small windows on top of the north cell block where Death Row was. Some of those boys up there would never get a pass like the one I clutched in my hand. I shivered as if a ghost had stepped beside me. I looked away from the little windows.

As the crowd of convicts grew under the shed you could see the facades alight as each convict adopted a look to discourage any confrontation. The hubbub of the crowd droned on as I stood among my cohorts.

I shook hands and said goodbye to the boys I thought I knew best. Most wished me luck and some punched me on the shoulder in the age-old checkout. I did not want to say I would never be back, that would jinx me for sure. I was looking for a sign, any kind of sign, that would tell me all would go well and I would make it on the outside this time.

'Industries work call!' the public address system blared. Convicts moved off to work down the hill as I stood there watching them go.

'Maintenance work call!' Again the speakers blared and more convicts moved down the hill to work in the maintenance shops.

'Laundry work call!' and convicts with little bundles of clothes moved out across the upper yard toward the laundry down the hill.

'Outside work crews!' That was the last of the morning work calls, as a handful of convicts moved off toward the sally port gate to work on the other side of the prison walls.

The crowd beneath the shed had thinned out considerably by now. I would have to wait for the loud speakers to announce pass call before I could move. I stood there contemplating this place of despair and human misery. It was an old prison, more than a hundred and fifty years old. The state would never close it as the real estate it sat on was priceless.

Another convict stood nearby with his own little shoe box and clutching his ticket to freedom also. We stood looking at each other, our facades cracked, and we smiled at one another.

I moved over to stand beside him. Listening, we both could hear the cooing of the pigeons in the steel girders overhead.

I started to speak to the convict to tell him about the sign. Just as I opened my mouth, he pointed upwards.

I looked up just in time to see a big grey and white pigeon ease his bottom clear of the girder. I stood dumbstruck as the pigeon shook his bottom above me and loosed a glutinous mass of stinking pale guano. It dropped with lightning speed. I could not move. My feet were glued to the pavement.

'Smack.' The mass of pale guano splattered against my forehead and down across my shoulders.

The other convict guffawed and slapped his knee. Stepping back out of the way he slowly shook his head from side to side.

It was then I knew, I finally had my sign.

'Pass call!' the public address system blared.

Steven King Ainsworth, Death Row, San Quentin, California

You hide where you can't

You,
With your mysterious embrace,
Your echoing infinity
And your mocking face.
Don't think you've fooled me.

Fear you?
Not I, know you too well.
You will not possess me,
Nor threaten me with hell.
Though, forth comes the horizon we must share.

Find you?
Yes, find you I will.
Though your discovery is a must,
It's of my choice still.
I will walk upon your ground and kiss you.

Love you?
No, love for you can't be.
You will caress me with chills,
But I will break free.
I laugh last, at you, the one called death.

Tracy A. Hansen, Death Row, Parchman, Mississippi

Burnt almonds

A burst of color and the vortex began to spin, a jumbled mass of scattered thoughts shot through my mind at incredible speed, my breathing became ragged and labored. Then as I gained some control of the quickly tripping synapse a picture began to emerge. The image cleared at the back of my skull.

There was no dignity in dying at the hands of a state ... any state! But it was my turn. I had exhausted all avenues of appeal. They had moved me to the death cell just hours before; the death watch took over, guards I have never seen before, none I knew ... all seemed so much larger than my six foot frame. The one outside the cell staring in intently, watching my every move. Another to the right by the death chamber door, sipping coffee from a styrofoam cup ... none the less alert and glancing up to peer at me. They did not try to talk to me as if I was a pariah.

Laying there on my last bed, my hands behind my head ... planning my last moves. Through the upper bars and across the way, the deadly eye of the gunrails weapon. Casually pointed my way, its deadly menace well known to me ... the man's face hidden in the shadows behind the rifle's stock ... the black eye raising and lowering minutely in mimic of the hidden gunner's respiration.

Buzzing, ringing, clangs, and muted shouts came through the thick cement walls. The sounds that bothered me the many years of delay. Keys turning, food slots banging, Spanish, English, Swahili, and other dialects of many voices shouting out in defiance from the cell blocks. A cacophony muffled and distant now from where I lay not fifteen feet from the gas chamber's door.

Acrid smells of antiseptic wash surrounded me. The death cell area was in full swing and I was just one of three who would go this week. The two before and now it was my turn center stage in the ritual of death ...

The two days before had gone quietly with little fuss. Their final statements of inane remarks. Meaningless gestures to victims and families. One's heartfelt reach for God no doubt fell on deaf ears and with tears he precedes me to ash.

I had decided that I would not go numbly down the path. I would not make a statement nor plea for clemency from the very system that had produced me as fodder for its now vast machine. My final moves, actions, would speak louder than words.

With my state issue five witnesses, I had provided the executioner's act with an audience that would not let this dance of death remain surreptitious from most. They would not allow the events of this morbid week to go unnoticed in the back pages of time. Where, in ignorance, the public could skip the account and not really think of the state that has to resort to killing its own citizens in address to its social deficiencies.

The hours, minutes, and seconds of this final day were tick-tocking away with speed. At some time, they brought my last meal and I wolfed down the gastronomical surprise, belching as the last remnants slid down to my stomach. When in death's grip, my sphincter relaxed and the contents of my viscera spilled out, the stench of faeces would add a sinister bouquet to assault the players in this rite when they entered the chamber after the deed was done. A pungent reminder of their part in the macabre.

Already the rubber tube protruded from my shirt front. Beneath where the medico had taped to my chest the stethoscope which would reverberate the sounds and finality of my demise. The criss-cross of adhesive tape exing me out.

Pacing back and forth to the hubbub around me, the time was coming close. The studied and practiced procedures of the death watch were in progress. Behind the death chamber door, the executioner was preparing the elements of the final brew. Little thuds and muted sounds filtered through the steel door.

Pacing back and forth, the cold cement chilling my stockinged feet. The black eye of the gunrails rifle muzzle following my movement. Back and forth, the death watch eyes followed me. Back and forth, back and forth. 'Calm down,' I told myself ... albeit in these moments of absolute terror, it was hard to do.

The Catholic priest came in, said some words, a jumble to me as the thudding of my heart became louder in my ears.

'It's time, it's time,' the death commander intoned. I stopped and made my move. The secreted razor blade came out and slashed my throat, and blood spurted as the jugular parted! Now my wrist and red appeared! Inside my arms, the blade rode, nipping the junctions of life's road there. Slinging my arms about, I flung the juice, splashing and splattering everyone, the walls and all.

Splotches of blood on the uniform of the minions of death as they charged into the cell to stop my act.

I smeared the blood on their skins, hair, and all over myself. Subdued, they 'cuffed me up. The medico wrapped the slashes up. They were pissed! Their nostrils flared in anger as they rushed me through the door into the chamber itself. They strapped me in quickly, as I spat on each.

The blinds on the windows flew up as they retreated out the gas chamber's door. Aghast, the witnesses gaped at the sight as the door shut and clamped tight. I swiveled my head to and fro to make the blood flow. It seeped through the wraps, darkening them with a moist red stain and dripping to the floor ... their eyes wide in horror, mine with madness.

Suddenly, my head sprang back as the gas hit my nose. I stiffened, my hands in fists, the knuckles white! I slumped forward and a shudder ran through my body ... the blood stopped, my struggle had ceased ... my eyes closed ... I relaxed ... the bitter sweet gas overtaking me ... peaches, apricots. No! Burnt almonds more like. This my last sense as my breathing ceased and life left me a shattered surreal hulk ... red, white and institutional green.

The vortex stopped spinning and the voices cleared ...

'Brewster! Brewster!' my name was called!

'What? What?' I gruffly replied.

'Brewster, Brewster, get four! get four!' the voice yelled.

'Get four? Get four?' confusedly I queried.

'Channel Four, they got you on Channel Four!' the voice screamed.

Automatically I sprang to the selector knob ... The TV tube brightened, my mug shot appeared, the newcaster's voice rang in my ear ...

' ... was given a full reversal today by the United States Supreme Court, ending a fifteen-year legal battle to execute him.'

Steven King Ainsworth, Death Row, San Quentin, California

Greetings from the grave
Death Row

I greet you there in the world of life
from here in the depths of a tomb
Words written in anger's grip
deep within Death's womb

To you who fought to put me here
may you forever ask yourself why
Were the votes really cause enough
to condemn me here to die

You play a game you cannot win
yet you cling to the useless act

Ignoring truth of what you know
and creating what you need as fact

To me it matters not
what your world will soon become
Built on lies and politics
to serve those you hide it from

But hear my words from the Gates of Hell
spoken with a dead man's breath
I curse your world of Justice's Lie
for with it you sanction my Death

Danny L. King, Death Row, Mecklenburg, Virginia

The escape from Death Row

Having spent six years and ten months on Death Row, I've seen many things, and experienced many things I never thought existed. But I was able to make the escape.

I was sentenced to death in September of '85 where I stayed up until July of '92. Many times I thought about escaping, but there were too many things to have to get through just to get to the fence, and once I would have gotten to the fence, death stood close by from within a tower just waiting for something to take place in order to be able to pull rank. Death was what I wanted to escape, not run into, so the thought was but a thought.

In November of '91, an officer came to my cell to tell me that I would be going on bench warrant the following morning. Immediately I knew what it would be for, but yet I was hoping that I would be wrong. Just as I thought, on the morning I was taken back to the county where my case was. I discovered that I was there to be given an execution date. I wasn't worried about anything, this was just to be done to force my next appeal, and my lawyers assured me of that. I called my aunt, who has been like a mother, father, brother and sister to me all my life. She was surprised to hear my voice on the phone and asked why was I back in Carthage. I tried to lie to her by telling her that I didn't know, but I couldn't live with lying to her, so I told her the truth. I felt like it wouldn't hurt her as much to lie to her than to tell the truth about why I was back in Carthage, Texas. We lost all of our family in death on my father's side of the family, which made me the only family she have. Although I have other family members on my mother's side of the family, my aunt and my son is the only family I have.

During the morning I was to be given the execution date, I went before the judge along with my lawyers. I glanced behind me a couple of times to see my aunt. I didn't want her to hear what was going to take place, but yet I knew that I couldn't tell her to leave. The judge asked me to stand, and then announced my execution date set for March 20, 1992. Afterward, he asked me if I had anything to say. I was trying to tell the judge that I first wanted to confer with one of my attorneys, but I could barely get the words to come out as I stood there feeling a numbness while shivering. The judge never understood me, so one of my lawyers intervened to explain what I was trying to say. It turned out that my lawyer preferred that I didn't say anything at that time.

My lawyers practically begged the judge not to give me the execution date, and assured him that they would file the next appeal by that date he was setting for my execution, but the judge turned deaf ears to their plea.

Afterward, I was allowed a visit with my aunt. I could tell that she was hurt by what just took place even though she was trying to hide it, and from the words she spoke, she felt like I would for sure be executed. One particular thing she stated as tears builded in the wells of her eyes was, 'If I don't see you on this side anymore, I hope to be able to see you on the other side ... in heaven.'

After my visit with my aunt, the officers scrambled to get the chains on me so they could take me back to Ellis 1 Unit. Once I returned, I didn't want anybody to know that I had an execution date, but it was discovered anyway, and written in one of the Death Row papers called *What's Happening*.

Three days before my execution date, I received a phone call from my lawyers telling me that I received a stay of execution. When we talk on the phone to anyone, there's always an officer on the other end listening to the conversation. The officer that was on the other end wrote a note to one of the higher officials telling him that my lawyer who I spoke with on the phone told me about the stay. So now I'm thinking that everything is all right, but at 6.30 the next morning, an officer came by to wake me to tell me that I had to pack my property so they could move me to the death watch cell. Apparently he got something mixed up somewhere, so I just told him okay so he would leave from in front of my cell. When he came back by and discovered that I hadn't gotten up to pack my property, he awaken me to ask me again. I then told him about my stay, but he claimed to not know anything about it, so I requested to speak with one of the ranking officers. I sit for a while waiting for one of the ranking officers to come by, but since it took some time, I went on and packed my property because I was sure that I wouldn't be in the death watch cell that long. I also didn't want them coming in to pack it – all they care about doing is stuffing your property in bags no matter how fragile it may be. Doing this is one of the main jobs they prefer not to do, and when they break something, your complaint is usually turned on deaf ears.

One of the ranking officers finally came by, but when he came by, I had most of my property packed, which there was no need for me to talk to him because I knew what was coming. Some kind of excuse about procedure.

After they moved me in the death watch cell, every thirty minutes an officer would come by, and whatever I was doing, they would write it down. Finally, one of the officers came by at approximately 5.00 p.m. the same day to tell me that I had a stay of execution. I tried my best to appear like what they were doing wasn't bothering me, but I was crushed. You see, they thrive on misery. When they (the officers) see they are getting to you, it makes them happy, and it causes them to want to push even more. It wasn't the fear of dying that bothered me, it was the fact that I realized that they've made mistakes before, and I was so afraid that they were going to make a mistake in my case. They've (the state) executed innocent people, and they've killed people who they discovered later had received a stay of execution.

In June of '92 during the afternoon hours, a couple of officers came by my cell to awaken me to tell me that my lawyers wanted me to call them. After getting up, one of the officers left from in front of my cell, and later returned. When he returned, he claimed that I was taking too long, and stated that he didn't have time for that and just walked off with the other officer following suit. I had all my clothes on, and was just washing my face when he returned, which was all I needed to do. The reason he didn't want to escort me to the office to make the call was because it was almost time for the shift to change.

The next morning I received a federal express letter from one of my attorneys. I set the package aside momentarily because I was afraid to open it to find unpleasant news, but my curiosity forced me to open it. I took the letter in hand without looking at it. When I did look at the letter, I glanced at it quickly, but my eye caught 'I'm pleased to ...'. I realized that it had to be some good news, so I focused my attention to the words that was in the letter and discovered that the Court of Criminal Appeals had vacated (overturned) my conviction. I began jumping, shouting and thanking God. I tried to contain myself because I realized that it wasn't final. Unpleasant news could possibly still be lying ahead since the prosecutor had fifteen days from the time of the ruling to request the Court of Criminal Appeals to reinstate the death penalty. Later I discovered that the prosecutor decided not to challenge the ruling, and requested for me to be taken back to the county jail.

Now I'm on a different unit with the life sentence. I'm able to move about instead of being locked down most of the day. I'm in the minimum part of a maximum security unit, and I now have a job working in the library as a clerk. At the moment, I'm helping sort the books out and get everything in order for opening. The first job I had was working outside keeping the sidewalk clean. The second one was helping in cleaning up a building along with some other guys. So far, I pretty much enjoy working in the library, which I know that things are going to get better after it opens. My only pay is good time. Good time is for instance: I've been incarcerated for over 8 years, but I have up to 20 something years good time.

I don't know what's to happen in the future. We have many things that we've endured in life, and have to endure. The majority of us count up all that we've been through and have to go through, but if we should spend more time counting our blessings, we wouldn't have time to count up all the unpleasant things in life. No one, not even God, ever told us that everything will be easy, and I'm very much a witness that it's not.

God, with his blessings, brought about my escape from Death Row!!!

Toby L. Williams, Abilene, Texas

The unseen, the forgotten

Graceful tall and swinging gates
Erupting voices of people's fates
The mystic air
Of life's despair
In a field of silence emanates,
All things here good and evil lay
With last words spoken in the day
This holy lot
That time forgot
In whistling winds and sky of gray,
Pale stones have deathly crowned
The heads of those beneath the mound
The breeze it cries
The silent sighs
Of restless souls chained to the ground,
The picket fence or wall of stone
Imprison those who live alone
And ring the chimes
Of their lifetimes
Whose memories grow unknown,
Against the wind the dead trees lean

In this lifeless sea of meadow green
Life must go on
But they aren't gone
We must remember those unseen.

Michael A. Williams, Death Row, San Quentin, California

Death penalty pilgrimage

to those who stride
out against the death penalty lighting the torch of
    conscience
POUND
with each step from starke, florida to atlanta, georgia
do in with your heels the distaste of death
does not give life
move forward
POUND
concrete ideologues dusty shoulders of
roads of lives walks life
   unite skeletons to flesh
   part the sea of red do like moses did
   journey this exodus for humanity
free fears
to talk about dying demoralization death destroying a
whole of this country
POUND
the gas chambers/rides on lightning/hempen
    neckties/
gurney hypocrisy/the anonymous single bullet to the
    heart
POUND
into oblivion that
hate which shouts the smut of revenge
with each step sing to the world of love
its poverty
POUND

upon arrival at the statehouse
(beneath that confederate flag which still flies)
DECLARE
'with death be done!'

Harold L. Otey, Death Row,
Nebraska State Penitentiary, Lincoln

Flowers

Bring my flowers to the cemetery's gate
The funeral procession, will not wait
And ask no questions, and you'll hear no lies
As the laughing thunder, rings through the skies
Just open your heart, with the skeleton key
And tell the world, what you think of me
Look for the answers, look in the stone
The one I'll lie under, all alone
See the past scenes, feel the cold
From the ice in my veins, down to the mold
Visits from skirts, visits from ties
Watching the people, say their goodbyes
Then comes the sound, the pitch of the pipes
And the chilling whistle, of the wind in the night
The box is closed, I rot inside
And in the process, a part of you died
You could've helped me, out of the haze
But the smoke from the fire, got in the way
Burned in your heart, burned in your glands
Burned by your friends, with blood on their hands
Gone forever, six feet down
With all of my memories, under the ground
But I will remember you, just the same
Despite the heartaches, and the pains
Cause I hold no grudges, my heart's not sour
Just say a prayer, and leave the flowers ...

Chris Tobin, Death Row, San Quentin, California

For my memory

Light a candle for my memory
in a quiet chapel by the sea;
as day drifts into dusky night,
cup it in your hands and hold me tight;
as the stars begin to softly shine,
blow out the flame as you call it mine;
I am gone, but in your heart I remain
as long as you whisper gently my name.
So light a chapel's candle by the sea –
hold it out as a guide for my memory.

Stephen Wayne Anderson, Death Row,
San Quentin, California

Appendix A
Letter from
President Bill Clinton

July 10, 1992

Friend
[blacked out] Broadmoor Avenue
Columbus, OH 43209

Dear Friend:

I appreciate your comments concerning the death penalty.
Decisions concerning executions and clemency are the most
difficult and soul searching choices any governor must make.

I have upheld the death penalty as the law of the state of
Arkansas. I support the use of the death penalty in cases
involving multiple murders or the killing of a police officer.

But the death penalty, by itself, is not enough to deter violent
crime. That is why I have proposed a detailed National Crime
Strategy that includes creating a national Police Corps to get
more policemen on the streets, restricting the sale of semi-
automatic assault weapons with no legitimate hunting purpose, and
providing drug treatment on demand.

Sincere and deeply held beliefs often differ on issues concerning
life and death. My own decision to uphold death verdicts was
reached after much prayer, study, and consultation. Thank you for
taking the time to write me.

Sincerely,

Bill Clinton
Bill Clinton

BC:sh

National Campaign Headquarters • P.O. Box 615 • Little Rock, Arkansas 72203 • Telephone (501) 372-1992 • FAX (501) 372-2292
Paid for by the Clinton for President Committee
Contributions to the Clinton for President Committee are not tax deductible.
Printed on Recycled Paper

239

Appendix B
LifeLines

Warren Wesley Summerlin is on Death Row in Arizona. He is illiterate. But he exchanges cassette tapes with Leonard Parsons in Britain. Leonard is blind; he is 93 and a member of LifeLines, whose members correspond with prisoners on Death Row in the USA.

LifeLines has grown from a solitary letter in 1987 into an organization of over 2,500 people writing to prisoners on Death Row in North America. LifeLines has also begun writing to Death Row prisoners in South Africa through a newly formed organization. Links are also being set up with Malaysia, where there is a large Death Row. Caribbean LifeLines, which has evolved in parallel with US LifeLines, writes to every prisoner on Death Row in the Caribbean. We have also started writing to a limited number of lifers in the USA.

The letters bring variety, colour and the outside world into the prison cells of those whom society has discarded. The following letter received recently from a prisoner in Texas asking for a pen-friend is typical: 'I don't have a family or anyone to help me or write me. That is why I am reaching out for friendship. I am intimidated real easy ... and I feel left out. I'm on the verge of giving up and the others guys pick on me.' As a PS he adds: 'Will someone please help restore my hope.'

Larry Stout, also in Texas, writes: 'LifeLines has brought life to me. Before belonging to LifeLines, I was thinking of giving up, tired of being alone. I still get lonely, but not like before. LifeLines has been terrific for everyone on Death Row. Our lives were almost programmed for a few years with death automatically at the end of the road – in between, nothing but a void, an empty shell. LifeLines has put life back into the shell.'

Because the prisoners give so much, the correspondence is often far more reciprocal and equal than those on this side of the Atlantic had ever imagined. Many start writing out of compassion or opposition to the death penalty, and find themselves drawn into close involvement with those they are writing to, to the point that many people – at least 50 – have now gone to the USA to visit 'their' prisoner.

At the same time, it needs to be borne in mind that many of the men have committed unspeakable crimes. What the correspondence brings out is the many facets to human beings; the fact that deprivation and pain have forced many of them to deny what they really feel; that many of them only discover who they really are on

Death Row; and that the death penalty provides no room for remorse, change or compassion. It is this, perhaps, that has been the secret behind LifeLines' growth. We have never advertised or actively sought publicity. People have responded to the human face of Death Row. We have much to learn from those who have been stripped of everything – dignity, self-esteem, possessions, love, support and hope – and who nevertheless emerge the stronger for the experience. Here are people who look death in the face daily, and who are thrust back on to their own, often pitifully developed, resources to an extraordinary degree.

Most of our LifeLines members come from the UK and Ireland, but we have letter writers in virtually every European country and in Japan, Hong Kong and Australia.

LifeLines is organized along state lines, with a 'co-ordinator' for each state. We issue a quarterly newsletter and hold two annual conferences a year, one in London and one elsewhere. Speakers have included the British Death Row lawyer Clive Stafford Smith, Sister Helen Prejean (a remarkable nun from Louisiana), Marie Deans (closely associated with the successful campaign against Joe Giarratano's execution in Virginia) and Bryan Stevenson, the brilliant young black lawyer based in Montgomery, Alabama (invited to the UK by Amnesty International in 1989).

LifeLines has a stamp shop and has counsellors to help people who run into problems (the most common being sexually charged letters and demands for money). There are now about a dozen regional groups throughout the country where LifeLiners can share the problems, rewards and joys of the letter writing in pub gatherings or in members' homes. Many firm friendships have been forged in the process.

LifeLines is not a political organization and deliberately does not campaign. It is purely a support organization. Many of its members, however, feel strongly about the death penalty, and out of this has arisen a separate campaigning body, Death Watch. Nor does LifeLines fund raise – although a charitable body, the Andrew Lee Jones Fund Limited, has just been set up. Its aim is to support British people through law school in the USA. Two LifeLiners, Hilary Sheard and Rachel Day, are at present pursuing their legal studies in the USA with a view to becoming Death Row attorneys.

A new development is that prisoners in the UK are beginning to write to prisoners on Death Row. This has largely come about because the book of prisoners' letters, *Welcome to Hell* (1991), is finding its way into prison libraries. One prisoner at the progressive Grendon Underwood Prison – a demanding therapeutic community, for which prisoners must volunteeer – is there only because of the encouragement and inspiration he has received from Sam Johnson on Death Row in Mississippi.

One of the chapters in *Welcome to Hell* provided the basis for the award-winning BBC *Everyman* programme 'LifeLine', first broadcast in February 1992. In response to the programme, which followed the short-lived correspondence between a retired music teacher in Britain and Ray Clark in Florida, LifeLines received a staggering 6,500 enquiries from people wanting to write. An article in *ME* magazine in 1992 produced a further 2,000 enquiries.

All this placed great strains on a tiny, backroom organization run solely by volunteers. Only about one in eight of those who enquire end up joining – mainly because LifeLines stresses the potential difficulties of the correspondence and asks people to think very carefully before committing themselves.

With the influx of new members in 1992, we built up an enormous waiting list. This has been worked off, and we are now in the reverse position: over 200 prisoners are waiting for pen-pals. Anyone interested in writing to a prisoner in the USA (or elsewhere) should send an SAE to: LifeLines, 96 Fallowfield, Cambridge, CB4 1PF.

Jan Arriens, founder and Chairman of LifeLines

Other LifeLines organizations

Caribbean LifeLines. c/o Andy McCoy, 5 Brent Gardens, Reading RG2 7SS.

Dutch LifeLines. c/o Herman Wijnhoven, Merwyckstraat 46, 5975 SL, Sevenum, The Netherlands.

Irish LifeLines. Secretary: Sue Milne, 19 Chalfont Part, Malahide, Co. Dublin, Ireland.

Malaysian LifeLines. c/o Caroline Robertson, 5 Vivian Close, Church Crookham GU13 OAJ.

Montsho LifeLines, South Africa. Robert Barnes, 42 Webster Avenue, Kenilworth CV8 2EJ.

Pinkpot. For befriending and corresponding with gay inmates on Death Row. c/o Derick Bird, 153 Swarthmore Road, Selly Oak, Birmingham B29 4NW.

Appendix C
The Andrew Lee Jones Fund

This fund exists to provide scholarships for individuals studying Law in the USA, with a view to practising in the field of capital defence.

The fund is named in memory of Andrew Lee Jones, who died in the electric chair in Louisiana on 22 July 1991. There are some doubts surrounding the evidence brought by the prosecution and mitigating factors which were not considered by the court. Better legal representation at his trial would have ensured that the jury heard all the relevant facts in considering whether to impose the death penalty.

A very large number of the 2,750 individuals on Death Row in the USA owe their plight to inadequate legal representation. Capital defence work is poorly paid, so very few well-qualified lawyers choose to specialize in this field. There is an urgent need for more highly motivated lawyers to prevent further miscarriages of justice.

It is extremely expensive to attend law school in the USA. Fees and living expenses vary between $20,000 and $30,000 per annum over a three-year course of study. US citizens may help with their costs by working part-time, but this is generally not permitted for foreign nationals on student visas.

The Andrew Lee Jones Fund therefore hopes to be able to offer scholarships to individuals who have obtained places at an American Bar Association approved law school on a needs basis. Students benefiting from the scholarship will be liable to repay the total sum advanced if they choose, on qualification, to specialize in a different field. Similarly, continued support from the fund depends on satisfactory performance throughout the student's course of study.

Patrons: Benjamin Zephaniah, John Mortimer, Ludovic Kennedy, Helena Kennedy QC, Michael Mansfield QC, Clive Stafford Smith, Paul Hamann, Lady Antonia Fraser, Bruce Kent, Ed Asner, A.S. Byatt.

Chairperson: Jane Officer; Secretary: Sophie Garner; Committee: Jane Palmer, Nick Davies, Mary Davies; Co-opted: Colin Williams.

Enquiries, legal matters: Sophie Garner, 199 Strand, London WC2R 1DR.

Fund-raising donations: Jane Officer, Hemyock Road, Selly Oak, Birmingham B29 4DG. Please make any donations payable to The Andrew Lee Jones Fund.

Afterword

Shortly after *Welcome to Hell* was published in 1991, a young man wrote to me saying that he had never read a more powerful or moving book. At the time, I wondered rather uncharitably whether he had read many books. Since then, many other people – including some prisoners in England – have written or told me that they feel exactly the same.

This book will, I am sure, fall into the same category. The prisoners' words have the power to cut like the lash one of the prisoners refers to from his own childhood. The prisoners make us yell, cry and laugh. They write like angels. Are these really the dregs of society? If so, how much more might we not all make of our lives?

Some prisoners crack under the isolation and deprivation. Fortunately there are those sufficiently strong to tell the tale. It is all the more powerful for being told from the inside; this is the prisoners' own authentic voice, and we may all be deeply grateful to Marie for having put the material together with such skill and sensitivity.

When a prisoner is executed, matters are arranged in such a way that no one individual bears responsibility. The judge passes sentence on behalf of society and in response to the jury's wishes; the State Governor signs the death warrant; the Warden instructs his staff; and the ritual is then broken down into a series of tiny steps each performed by different people, so that at the end no one person – and everyone – is responsible for the final deed.

So also with the prisoners. In nearly all cases, the deeds that put them on Death Row can be traced back through a long series of events and a long line of individuals. These pages show how pain and bewilderment are passed on from one generation to another. They show how the murderer is, as it were, the final actor in a complex chain of social forces. The murderer, too, is victim; we are all responsible.

Despite the injustice, the torture of their existence, the unquestioned 'cruel and unusual punishment', the lack of any outlet for remorse or atonement, the denial of constitutional and human rights, and the dehumanizing terror of their existence, the men change, reach out and display far more insight, compassion and sensitivity than the system that holds them. I am reminded of Churchill's words: 'One of the unfailing tests of the civilization of any country is an unfaltering faith that there is a treasure, if only you can find it, in the heart of every man.'

Jan Arriens, editor of Welcome to Hell

Last words

I regard the death penalty as a savage and immoral institution which undermines the moral and legal foundations of a society. A state, in the person of its functionaries, who like all people are inclined to making superficial conclusions, who like all people are subject to influences, connections, prejudices and egocentric motivations for their behaviour, takes upon itself the right to the most terrible and irreversible act – the deprivation of life. Such a state cannot expect an improvement of the moral atmosphere in its country. I reject the notion that the death penalty has an essential deterrent effect on potential offenders. I am convinced that the contrary is true – that savagery begets only savagery.

Andrei Sakharov, prisoner of conscience, USSR

The deliberate, institutionalized taking of human life by the state is the greatest conceivable degradation to the dignity of the human personality.

Former US Supreme Court Justice Arthur Goldberg, quoted in The Boston Globe, *16 August 1976*

As one whose husband and mother-in-law have died the victims of murder assassination, I stand firmly and unequivocally opposed to the death penalty for those convicted of capital offenses. An evil deed is not redeemed by an evil deed of retaliation. Justice is never advanced in the taking of a human life. Morality is never upheld by a legalized murder.

Coretta Scott King